From Selfies
to Selflessness

From Selfies
to Selflessness

Improving Student Self-Esteem
through Mentoring

Cary Knox

ROWMAN & LITTLEFIELD
Lanham • Boulder • New York • London

Published by Rowman & Littlefield
An imprint of The Rowman & Littlefield Publishing Group, Inc.
4501 Forbes Boulevard, Suite 200, Lanham, Maryland 20706
www.rowman.com

86-90 Paul Street London EC2A 4NE

British Library Cataloguing in Publication Information Available

Library of Congress Cataloging-in-Publication Data

Names: Knox, Cary, author.
Title: From selfies to selflessness : improving student self-esteem through
    mentoring / by Cary Knox.
Description: Lanham : Rowman & Littlefield, [2021] | Includes bibliographical
    references.
Identifiers: LCCN 2021016113 (print) | LCCN 2021016114 (ebook) |
    ISBN 9781475860399 (cloth) | ISBN 9781475860405 (paperback) |
    ISBN 9781475860412 (ebook)
Subjects: LCSH: Mentoring in education—United States. | Selflessness
    (Psychology)—United States. | Self-esteem in adolescence—United States. |
    Internship programs—United States. | Internet and teenagers—United States. |
    Social media and society—United States.
Classification: LCC LB1731.4 .K64 2021 (print) | LCC LB1731.4 (ebook) |
    DDC 371.102—dc23
LC record available at https://lccn.loc.gov/2021016113
LC ebook record available at https://lccn.loc.gov/2021016114

♾ ™ The paper used in this publication meets the minimum requirements of
American National Standard for Information Sciences—Permanence of Paper for
Printed Library Materials, ANSI/NISO Z39.48-1992.

This book is dedicated to **John William Redman.** *A former student who gave his teacher a newly found purpose in life.*

Contents

Preface

Rewriting a Child's Story

As a teacher in a public school for the past three decades, I have lived to hear countless stories that each child brings in from their home. Many of these stories are wonderful and bring great joy to share, especially when I get to see my students transforming into successful and compassionate adults. I recently had the honor of watching one of my former students—after spending five years overcoming the trauma of his younger brother's death and an Oppositional Defiant Disorder (ODD) diagnosis—graduate from basic training in the US Army.

But for every wonderful story, there seems to be a story with a uniquely sad twist. Students share these stories with us in a variety of ways, but the story itself remains. Sometimes the story is shared through a family member or a community member. Sometimes we are notified by agencies outside of the home that are trying to help. Sometimes the child shares this information with us and then we choose what to do next. Sometimes the story is never shared; then, the child continues to hurt, fall further behind in school, or struggle in social settings.

It can be difficult for a teacher to know each individual child's story and how to address it, especially when teachers are already consumed with so much responsibility, often teaching 30 or more students at one time. The Links of Strength mentoring program takes this responsibility, generally given to the classroom teacher, and gives it to a caring mentor within the school's community.

For many years, I heard these sad stories discussed among students in the hallways or teachers in the break room. Despite the sympathy I felt for the child, I didn't know what concrete steps I could take to help. Part of my problem was not knowing how to intervene within the framework of a regular school day. Like most teachers, I would show up to school and immediately head to my room and wait for the children to arrive, or I would have breakfast with my fellow teachers in the cafeteria.

Many teachers are so overwhelmed with daily tasks that taking on anything more is unrealistic. But for the teachers out there that do have the time, ability, or mental energy to do more, I realized that the opportunity was there for us. I really started to think about the wasted time at the beginning of each school day and how we could better serve students with the extra time. Giving your undivided time to a child is an opportunity to bond and develop trust. Our own story, a child's story, or a coworker's story can at times be filled with successes and failures.

In 2008, I developed a concept called Links of Strength; when we connect with those around us who inspire us and give us strength, we all become stronger as a result. When starting Links of Strength, my goal was to help others identify other people in their lives who provided them with a stable source of strength and encouragement.

For example, some of my own Links of Strength include my wife, my children, my grandchildren, and Jesus Christ, all of whom inspire and motivate me every day. While I have used scripture to explain Links of Strength to other Christian audiences, the program and concept can apply to students in public schools regardless of religious background; it's all about recognizing those we're thankful for and linking up to provide support for one another.

As an educator, I want to ensure that each of my students has their own set of Links of Strength, both at home and at school. Often, children are let down by family, life, and individuals in charge of their story, and need someone in the school setting to provide the strength. "Linking Up" is the term we use at school when we provide strength with high school students, faculty, staff, or community members. When you choose to Link Up, you become a Link of Strength for another person. Linking up has become a common and popular phrase at our school as it reflects on the positive vibe it has created. This positive reaction has also been noticed by professionals throughout the state and has provided opportunities for the message to be shared.

Many children going to school across the United States and in the world fight a long list of issues. Some of the problems I have seen students dealing with in my 30 years as a teacher include:

- Homelessness
- Broken homes due to divorce or family conflict
- Drugs inside the home
- Verbal and physical abuse
- Inconsistent discipline from parents and exposure to profanity in the home
- Poverty
- No one to listen
- Broken promises from family members
- Lack of love
- Loneliness, often resulting from overuse or misuse of phones and social media

As a teacher, I am starting to see the reliance on social media and technology as a growing problem with families, especially our youth. As students become more captivated by their phones, often unable to stay off of them in class, and adults—including parents and teachers— spend more and more time outside of the classroom on social media, we all start to forget one key component of human connection: the empathy that results from face-to-face interactions. Children that come from homes of emotional disrepair need teachers, students, and staff to put their phones down and act.

This book, *From Selfies to Selflessness: Improving Student Self-Esteem through Monitoring* will address these issues and give concrete steps that teachers, students, and parents can take to prioritize human interaction first, even in today's world of texting and selfies.

Not all students or teachers are willing or able to give up their free time in the morning or at the end of the day, as the Link Up program requires. But some are, and we need to encourage those people to Link Up and listen. Identifying weaknesses and providing strength in our schools is more important now than at any time in history.

At my school, we have spent the past five years implementing and revising the Link Up mentorship program, which other schools around us are now adopting as well. One school in particular has given students school credit through an internship: high school students will receive credit for an elective class if they spend time mentoring a younger at-risk student. Our mentors listen to and build strong relationships with the most at-risk children in our schools.

The phone and social media onslaught will not be going away; if the past few years have shown us anything, it's that the use of cell phones, the internet, and social media will only be getting stronger. Instead of ignoring technology, pretending like it doesn't exist, or trying to get rid of it, we need to address the root causes of the issues that it is amplifying. Those who have the time, opportunity, and ability to provide strength to others should not waste this opportunity.

In our program, we start by identifying at-risk children, such as those whose families are dealing with an issue like divorce, poverty, drug use, or any other major conflicts. Our team of mentors, which includes teachers, administrators, staff members, and high school students, will each pair up with one child, whom they give their undivided attention every morning.

In our school, the mentor and mentee meet at 7:45 every morning and begin their day together. The first order of business is to make sure the child has eaten breakfast. If not, the mentor ensures that breakfast is provided. After breakfast, the mentor goes to the child's classroom to check on unfinished schoolwork. If all work is done, the mentor and mentee will read a book together, have a conversation, or simply share each other's company.

Until the school day officially begins at 8:20 a.m., the mentee can talk with their mentor about any topics of concern. At the end of the day, from 2:50–3:05, the mentor will help the mentee organize and prepare for the evening and next day.

Sharing time and developing trust and friendship helps children feel comfortable at school, which provides more confidence. The relationship between the mentor and mentee also helps the mentor realize the importance of helping others. This program is a win-win and has proven to work at each school that has implemented it.

No matter how old we are, we all have a story to tell. As adults, we have the means to change our story, but many times a child does not. Linking Up through mentoring gives us a chance to rewrite a child's story and put them on the track to a successful and happy life. We have the time and the human capital to make a difference. This book aims to inspire you to Link Up with others in need and to help you and the children in your life move from selfies to selflessness.

Acknowledgments

Several people played vital roles in making this far-fetched dream, of publishing a book, a reality.

- My wife **Kellie** for her love, timely research, and for pushing me across the finish line.
- My editor **Savy Leiser** for her brilliance and support.
- My agent **Cyle Young** for finding the right publisher and for his consistent belief in me as a writer.
- My friend **Bev Johns** for guidance.
- My Publisher Rowman and Littlefield
- **Tom Koerner**—Vice President and Publisher for Education Issues
- **Carlie Wall**—Managing Editor
- My children **Ryan** (Amy), **Sean** (Abbey), **Allyson** (Cade) and **Adam** (Victoria). My beautiful grandchildren **Ava, Scarlett, Indie, James, Augie, and Jude.**
- **My Lord and Savior for never leaving my side.**

Introduction

What Is the Link Up Internship?

While internships are not a requisite for college or trade school admittance, the truth is that completing one will often give high school students a leg up when it's time to move on from high school. At a minimum, interning gives teenagers the opportunity to get up close with something they find interesting, no matter the industry.

An amazing component to early internships is that they allow students a glimpse into their future. They get an inside look at how this particular field operates to determine whether or not it's something they can see themselves doing for the long-term. If it's not something they like, at least they know then.

HOW DO INTERNSHIPS HELP TEENS?

In many cases, high school students haven't had much responsibility outside of school. Attending class and doing homework is important, but it's not designed as a real-world experience. With an internship, they are expected to behave like a professional rather than a student. Interacting with other professionals and dealing with job-related stressors are the norm, helping them learn a little bit more about what their post-school life will be like.

For the internship to be successful there must be clarity of tasks. According to the Wisconsin Center for Education Research, students must understand the work, expected deliverables, and performance criteria.[1] Task variety, feedback, and opportunities to interact with professionals are important for intern satisfaction. In a mentoring internship, the intern needs to feel that their role is meaningful not only to the mentee, but also for them as a mentor.

According to Matthew Hora, Matthew Wolfgram, and Samantha Thompson—researchers for the Center for Research on College-Workforce Transitions from the University of Wisconsin-Madison—some studies have shown that people who participated in internship programs have greater job satisfaction. They go on to say that some argue that this is due to the reduction of "entry shock" to full-time duties.[2]

What do we know about the impact of internships on student outcomes? Internships are the first time when many students are in an environment where they intend to spend most of their professional lives. They will meet co-workers and administrators who are interested in the same things they are and who have successfully made a career out of it. The connections made may be an employer in the future.

The internship helps the interns make long-lasting friendships. Before students head off for college or begin their trade, branching out from your high school friends and meeting people with shared career interests is healthy. Some of these friendships will last a lifetime and will always be a source to seek out when they have questions about their field of choice. Many of their contacts will have similar life goals and the chance to share this time is valuable.

BENEFITS OF THE LINK UP PROGRAM FOR INTERNS

Most high school internships interfere with a busy high school student's schedule. Whether students are athletes, musicians, artists, or members or any other time-consuming extra-curricular activity, squeezing in one more duty can seem legitimately impossible. Finding the right internship is important for students with busy schedules.

The Link Up Mentoring Internship is perfect for students with busy schedules. The schedule for all interns occurs within the framework of the school day. For some schools that share the same building, the intern's tasks can occur at any time throughout the day. At some schools, students take classes that are not necessarily a good fit for them but it is the only thing available for that time slot. For this student, the Link Up internship is a real advantage over taking a class they are not interested in.

For the building down the road or simply around the block, the time spent interning will be at the start of the school day or at the end of the school day. Making time for selfless acts is perfect for this internship.

THE LINK UP INTERNSHIP IN ACTION

In January of 2019, team from the Link Up Program was invited to speak at the Illinois Council for Children with Behavioral Disorders in Chicago, Illinois. At this event, the opportunity was given to share the vision of mentoring socially at-risk children and how to best go about it. The event brought thousands of teachers from all over the state to learn more about the need to help children that are lost and falling further behind.

Teachers and administrators are searching for ways to reach these children within the framework of the traditional school day. Two teachers in particular were inspired by the Link Up message and took their excitement back to their administrators. Charleston High School, from the east side of Illinois, was eager to hear more.

In April of 2019, the original Link Up team from the Meredosia-Chambersburg school district was invited to come share the Link Up vision three hours east in Charleston, Illinois. The program was gaining traction and the excitement was building

Charleston High School is located across the street from Eastern Illinois University and currently serves over 800 students. The school was ready to share the resources that walked the hallways of the high school in a meaningful and life-changing way. In their handbook, Charleston already had a course description that dealt with interning. With the school being so close to the university, students often interned on the Eastern Illinois campus.

Charleston's internship class allowed each child to receive two high school credits while also providing their presence to a child in need. Down the road from the high school sits Carl Sandburg Elementary, which serves first through third grade students in the Charleston School District.

Because Link Up Mentoring Program focuses on the socially at-risk child, Charleston School District was able to use the following course description to Link Up some high school students with teacher-identified at-risk children.

INTERNSHIP (54510954610 22998A000 11,12 GL 18 WEEKS 2CR.

Prerequisite: None. Internship is a volunteer work experience with any local business. Students are required to volunteer a minimum 7 ½ hours per week. Students should receive on the job training through observation and various training experiences at the job site. Students will be required to complete a weekly time sheet, a midterm assignment, and an end of the semester assignment. Additional requirements may be added throughout the semester. Good School attendance is required for this class.

With an obvious need at Carl Sandburg and the resources just down the road, the district was ready to assist. Using the above course description, students signed up, children were identified, and the work began.

The Link Up mentors arrived at 7:30 every morning and signed in at the office, relinquishing their phone to get to work. Each mentor was assigned to a specific room and teacher. The mentor would wait with the teacher until the identified child arrived at school. Upon arrival of the student, the mentor, at the direction of the teacher, would begin the mentoring process.

The original Link Up team from Meredoisa-Chambersburg kept in constant contact with the Charleston School District and was so pleased to hear of the early success. Mentees showed major social progress, so more mentors were added for the second semester of school. Arriving at 7:30 and leaving at 9:00, five days a week, was making a tremendous impact on the lives of struggling children. Upon leaving the school, the mentors would sign out, pick up their phone, and head back down the road to finish their day at the high school.

Beyond the obvious successes at Charleston, the Link Up Program made note of some items for concern and improvement. Many times, the teacher in charge was so overwhelmed with their class size that they were starting to rely on the mentor as a classroom aide rather than solely a mentor to their assigned child. The mentoring program's primary focus is on the one child that has been identified. If the child is absent, then the mentor will serve the teacher and or other needy students in the room.

The second concern related to some of the issues that mentee children were facing. Asking a high school-aged student to mentor a child with behavioral needs that require a trained professional is not advisable. You are setting up the mentor to fail and the time spent is wasted. The socially at-risk student is someone that needs a listening ear, companionship, and someone to help them build some self-esteem.

Lives were changed in positive ways at Carl Sandberg and by continuing the Link Up Program and by making some subtle changes the future is bright. It's all about finding that life-changing link.

NOTES

1. Hora, Wolfgram, & Thompson. "What do we know about the impact of internships on student outcomes?" Center for Research on College-Workforce Transitions, Research Brief #2. 2017. http://ccwt.wceruw.org/documents/CCWT-report-Designing-Internship-Programs.pdf

2. Ibid.

Section 1

HOW MENTORING
CREATES SELFLESSNESS

Chapter 1

Learning Selflessness in a Self-Absorbed World

All people share a common link: everyone has a story to tell, filled with joy, despair, failure, and triumph. Every story differs to a degree, but each is equally important to tell. When encouraging selflessness and empathy in young people, it can be particularly important to share the stories of students who are already exemplifying these traits and to honor the student. Take, for example, Ann, the first recipient of the Links of Strength Award.

At 7:00 p.m. on a Wednesday night in 2015, a mother dropped her children off at the children's fathers house for a visit—a common occurrence for kids whose parents have split up. However, rarely does the mother disappear, never to be seen again. After dropping off the three children at their dad's house, the mother took off for Florida with her new boyfriend. To this day, four years later, little to no communication has been shared between the mother and her abandoned children.

The father remained loyal to his children, but he couldn't perform all the duties necessary to keep the family moving in the right direction. Early every morning before the kids would awaken, he would head off to work. Left at home were three children aged eleven, nine, and seven. Not only were they dealing with the loss of their mother, but they were also dependent on each other to get ready for school. Once again, this is not totally uncommon, especially among children who have a single parent. However, not many eleven-year-old children are left to take care of a seven-year-old sister who is totally blind.

The oldest of the three, Ann, was left to care for her siblings and provide strength each and every day. Ann's younger sister, Beth, attended a school for visually impaired students, which was 30 minutes away and required bus transportation each morning. Ann, who was only eleven at the time, prepared Beth for school every morning and made her breakfast in time to board the bus. After Beth boarded the bus, Ann turned her attention to herself and their brother to get ready for school.

Given the task of an adult, Ann never wavered; she acted as a source of strength for her siblings, even though she was an abandoned child just like they were. After doing this for four years, she was honored by the Meredosia-Chambersburg School District as the very first winner of the Links of Strength award. Staff and faculty shared her story with everyone at a school assembly. When faculty called her to the gym floor, the student body rose to their feet in applause. There were tears in the eyes of every person in the gym

Now fifteen, Ann is a member of the Link Up mentorship program, and she provides strength and selflessness to younger students every day. Teaching students the importance of selflessness, the Link Up mentorship program is rewriting a child's story one day at a time.

A common complaint among adults is that Generation Z can be too self-absorbed: too wrapped up in their cell phones, too focused on social media, too focused on themselves. Some teachers might laugh at the possibility of today's high school students committing to a completely selfless mentorship program.

Ann's story shows that this isn't true, and it's not the only story. Before Ann received her Links of Strength award, another student had shown selflessness as well: she reported what was going on at Ann's home to her teachers. One of Ann's friends approached her teachers to explain everything that Ann was doing for her sister, phrasing it to show how proud she was of her friend and to ensure Ann received recognition for her hard work.

This exchange showed the compassion in our youth and how it could be used at school everyday throughout the school year. If done properly, we could change our school and many others, one selfless student at a time.

Walking through the hall of a high school building can be chaotic if not scary—early mornings can make teachers feel like they're lost in a sea of loud teenagers laughing at jokes they don't understand, bright cell phone screens everywhere, loud music coming out of headphones, and arguments about the latest teen drama happening all around.

However, after giving Ann her award and implementing the Link Up mentorship program, the hallways of Meredosia-Chambersburg are filled with students stopping teachers to say hello, talking with their mentees, and having face-to-face conversations.

Recognizing a student like Ann for her hard work doesn't only reward a student for selflessness; it also incentivizes students to look out for each other. Without Ann's help, a student like her sister, Beth, may have fallen through the cracks.

Identifying the children socially at-risk is the first step to directed intervention. Next, identifying the students who will serve as mentors and provide this strength is vital in the success of the Link Up program.

Understanding the program and getting input from the entire faculty is very important. Many teachers are almost constantly searching for ways to assist the socially at-risk students, but lack answers to how. No heart is bigger than that of a teacher, and if shown the way, a teacher can impact a child's life every day.

When the Link Up mentorship program first began, there was some concern among teachers that students would not find the program appealing. Faculty worried that students giving up their free time, which many spend on Instagram, YouTube, Snapchat, or texting, would be too much to sacrifice.

According to a 2018 Pew Research Poll, 95 percent of all teens have access to a smartphone and 45 percent say they are online constantly. Pew also found 85 percent of teens using YouTube, 72 percent using Instagram, 69 percent using Snapchat, 51 percent using Facebook, and

32 percent using Twitter on a daily basis. And let's face it, it's not just students; teachers, staff, parents, and community members are consumed with this as well.

See, this program, in many ways, is a result of social media defining everyone. When people get used to receiving "likes" on social media for every positive action, providing selfless duties without getting an immediate reward might not feel that rewarding by comparison. Thus, teachers worried that high school students would not rally behind a cause that took a lot of effort without any instant gratification. The results, however, were a pleasant surprise.

Giving up 30 minutes every morning and every afternoon might not seem like much, but in today's world that is an eternity of time. Surrendering your phone upon arrival at school to do selfless work with others can be a shock to your system. No likes, no shares, no comments about how great your life seems to be. Your reward is simply the gratification of providing your time in a selfless manner to a child in need. You may not see the notifications on your phone, but you will feel the gratification in your heart!

Providing strength for a child and teaching selflessness in a selfish world is worth the time. Linking Up defines a kid's willingness to give his/her time without any compensation beyond the gratification you feel in your soul!

Takeaways for Teachers:

- The key to starting a successful mentorship program is selflessness, both on your part and the part of your students.
- Selflessness comes from the desire to help another person without any expected reward; it's important to let go of the need for instant gratification.
- While it may seem like teenagers are too wrapped up in technology and social media to learn selflessness, if you give them the opportunity to show compassion, they might pleasantly surprise you!

Chapter 2

Don't Wait for Them; Go Find Them

Most teachers, as mandated reporters, know what signs to look for in a suffering student. However, not all students show outward signs of trouble at home. The Link Up program encourages teachers and mentors to be proactive about finding students to help, rather than waiting for a disaster to happen.

At Meredosia-Chambersburg, the shop teacher is a retired pastor. He had been counseling the parents of two children in the school, and he was aware of the couple's plans to officially separate. He, along with other teachers in the school who knew of the couple's impending divorce, spent the week worried about how it would affect those students.

One of the children affected, Jennifer, was a high school mentor in the Link Up program. Her younger sister, Amanda, who was in second grade, wasn't as well prepared to handle her parents' divorce as Jennifer was. Amanda became angry at everyone. She refused to talk to her teachers or classmates, and after a few weeks, she was beginning to fail her classes.

Jennifer realized that her younger sister needed a support network during this time. She needed to get her sister involved in the Link Up program as a mentee. Because Jennifer was already serving as a mentor, she suggested Linking Up her younger sister with another mentor in the program.

The student chosen to Link Up with Amanda was a good listener and had a caring, empathetic personality. We began the process of Linking the two together, and the results were immediate. The child's anger toward others went away and the healing process was well underway. This child also expressed to others that Linking Up made her feel special exactly when she needed it most.

Sometimes adults can recognize a child's sadness before the child even knows what they're feeling. Amanda's story is just one out of a school building full of stories. It's important to remember that a child's story is never finished; many parts of a child's life will change over the years as they grow up.

Teachers have the power to help write that story rather than letting that story tell itself, and the Link Up program is there to help steer that story in a more positive direction. In today's world of unsettled families there is no time to wait for the child to find an adult; by looking for children who may need extra support in their life, you can help give that child strength.

Often, identifying these students can be difficult for a teacher with an already overwhelming workload. Very few professions are harder than that of a teacher. Emotional stress takes its toll and teachers feel overwhelmed. For that reason, it's common for teachers to reach their classroom in the morning, sit at their desk, and wait for the bell to send the students their way. A teacher might use that time to set up their classroom, relax before the school day starts, or even check their own Facebook, Instagram, or Twitter accounts. In many ways, adults and students are captive to the same problems.

The Links of Strength movement, and the subsequent Link Up mentorship program, was born from teachers using time before school starts to plan and execute it. Many of these teachers had previously spent time on their phones, but realized that time could be put to better use. This book aims to help you identify and use those spare moments of time to better help students, and to encourage your students to do the same.

Think of the free human capital that walks through the doorways of every school across the United States. According to the National Center for Education Statistics there are 132,853 schools in the United States. Every year, at about the same time, school starts and teachers head to work. With over 3 million teachers driving to work and 15 million students attending public high schools, enough "free" human capital exists to make a difference.

This book, the Links of Strength message, and the Link Up mentorship program will direct this free human capital in places that will have the greatest impact humanly possible. Keep in mind, this program may not be right for every teacher or every student, and that's all right. Participation in the program should be voluntary and should only involve the students and teachers who feel that they have the emotional availability to devote to the project.

Many schools already have guidance counselors or social workers, but that is just one person, often having to manage many students, and often only able to devote allotted appointment time to working with that student. While those roles are necessary and effective, it's not always enough for children identified as socially at-risk.

This program is not intended to replace the help of social workers, therapists, licensed counselors, and law enforcement when needed—such as in cases of abuse. However, this program *is* meant to help students build a network of peers and allies to rely on for strength.

For many elementary classroom teachers, their job is overwhelming. They know and recognize that some students need extra love and attention. They want to provide, but trying to manage time in a classroom of 25–30 won't allow this to happen. It breaks their heart and they welcome the added help from high school students and other teachers that have voluntarily chosen to Link Up and help change a child's school year and maybe their life.

An important component of this program is that it's FREE! So far, the Link Up program has used none of the budget in the Meredosia-Chambersburg district where it was first implemented, nor has it cost teachers any money. With schools hurting for money and cutting many extracurricular programs all around the country, it's important to have a program that doesn't require money to run; one that will always be at our disposal, regardless of financial constraints.

Linking Up a student, staff member, or teacher every morning and afternoon with a socially at-risk student is too important to ignore. Socially at-risk students suffer with low self-esteem, learning or behavioral disabilities, or past abuse. Teachers and other adults hear about "at-risk youth," whether it's from the anti-drug PSAs seen on TV commercials or the discussions among adults in the teachers' lounge.

But for every time you hear about the abstract concept of at-risk kids, how often are you stopping to take concrete steps to help an at-risk child in your own community? This program is designed to help you identify those problems that you already know are happening and develop concrete steps to move forward.

The answer is right in school buildings all over the United States! Free human capital arrives every morning with goodness in their hearts and a selfless attitude. Every school is already filled with tons of people capable of selflessness, as long as teachers and students know how to tap into that.

Through the help of the classroom teacher, faculty, and mentors involved in the Link Up program are able to identify the children who need help—such as those who have low school attendance, who struggle with anger issues, or who we know have a history of violence in their home—and immediately serve them throughout the school year.

In a time when schools are bereft of money and programs are being cut in many places, it's necessary to use resources already within the school building to address our children. The resources are in the building and ready to serve!

Many teachers already have to arrive at school before 8 a.m. anyway, and many stay late in the afternoon. Free human capital in every school building in the United States just waiting for someone to point them in the right direction. Free human capital is priceless.

Takeaways for Teachers:

- Teachers should be proactive in searching for students who may need an extra support network.
- A mentorship program like Link Up should be voluntary and can be implemented with no financial cost.
- The best resource teachers, students, staff, and faculty have in a school is each other.

Chapter 3

Like, Comment, or Share

The same brain phenomenon that happens when a person eats Rocky Road Ice Cream or makes the game-winning shot also occurs when teenagers see hundreds of "likes" on their own photos: a dopamine fix. The "like" button, debuting on Facebook in 2009, has created feedback that many covet. The need for affirmation and acceptance, in many ways, determines who you are. The more "likes" you get, the more "love" you feel. By contrast, being ignored, "not liked" can be psychologically devastating.

Social media allows teens to create online identities, network, and communicate with others. Often, the ability to network can provide teens with needed support, especially to those that suffer from not fitting in. Meeting others from far reaching geographical areas, staying in touch with friends who have moved away, and communicating with relatives in other parts of the country can all make social media worthwhile and beneficial for kids. Because information circulates quickly online, social media also allows teens to stay up-to-date on current events happening in the world around them. Social media has many benefits—when used in moderation.

THE IMPACT OF SOCIAL MEDIA

Today's teenager spends a shocking nine hours a day with digital technology. This time includes entertainment uses—like streaming videos online or playing video games—as well as educational uses like reading the news or doing homework. It also includes using social media apps like Instagram, Facebook, Twitter, YouTube, TikTok, and Tumblr.

Many teenagers recognize the need to cut back their time on social media, but frequently find themselves drawn back in. Harvard Medical School reports that a young person's brain lacks a fully developed self-control system to help them with stopping this kind of obsessive behavior.[1] Social media poses a real threat of addition, especially to kids and teens.

RISKS OF SOCIAL MEDIA ABUSE

Social media also allows increased access to cyberbullying, which can lead to depression and suicidal thoughts. Even subconsciously, kids begin to crave the "likes" of their peers; posts that receive no "likes," comments, or positive attention can result in feelings of inadequacy. Having thousands of supposed "friends," but never connecting with them on a personal level, can exacerbate feelings of loneliness. Overuse of social media also increases the risk of cyberbullying.

Cyberbullying also involves the sending, posting, or sharing of private information causing embarrassment or humiliation. Some cyberbullying crosses the line and becomes criminal behavior. Despite the absence of physical contact or audible threats, cyberbullying can be even more traumatizing than other forms of bullying. Through multiple forms of social media and electronic devices, bullying can now be viewed by all of a child's friends, family, and others. Due to this, the embarrassment, shame, and other more serious consequences of bullying can become even more severe.

SOCIAL MEDIA ADDICTION AND DEVELOPING BRAINS

The obsession with receiving "likes" and positive affirmations online has taken some strange and sad twists since the "like" button debuted in 2009. Likes, comments, and shares are all about the feeling of acceptance. Due to this constant need for affirmation, the world has witnessed family tragedy and individual suffering at the hands of social media.

The effect of screen time on brain development is not fully understood. Experts are concerned that it does affect the ability to pay attention. According to the American Psychological Association, heavy smartphone usage has been associated with preferences for quick rewards. Feedback from social media has been associated with activations in reward-related brain regions, and has been shown to be weakly correlated with negative indicators of psychological well-being.[2] Screen time has also been associated with childhood obesity, sleep disruption, and language and social-emotional delays.

ADULTS AREN'T IMMUNE

Social media addiction can affect adults in a similar way as children; while most adults' brains are fully formed, social media can still take a toll on an adult's parenting style. When a parent is not engaging with the child because he or she is on their phone a lot, or when a parent regularly gives their young child an iPad as a distraction or reward, the parent and child are missing out on an important opportunity for bonding.

Many times, the child feels lonely and lacks the feeling of belonging when their caregiver overuses social media. Parents, just like teenagers, are chasing similar satisfaction through social media and its adversely affecting their ability to parent.

THE LOSS OF HUMAN CONNECTION

With a screen separating two people, some find it easier to insult their peers in ways they wouldn't do in person. The range of cyberbullying can be wide, from small insults due to the competitive nature of counting "likes" and comments, to all-out torment that has caused some children to take their own life. Often, cyberbullies may not know the effect of their words on another person because of the screen between them.

So much of social media is about control, good or bad. Many people like to control the image they put forth online, whether through edited photos on Instagram or positive life updates on Facebook. The problem is, by curating our images so heavily, we lose out on the real impact of human connection: the inflection in someone's voice, the look in their eyes, the energy of a discussion.

The necessity of in-person connection became even more evident when schools had to shut down for COVID-19. Student safety is always the top priority, especially in a worldwide pandemic, which is why online instruction is an adequate substitute in the meantime—though it still misses the full experience. Especially during a pandemic that requires social distancing, students need to monitor how much time they spend on text or photo-based social media; at the very least, a one-on-one discussion over video conferencing software can be a halfway decent substitute.

FINDING SELF-WORTH THROUGH SELFLESSNESS

Overuse of social media encourages teens to focus on *their* image and the attention *they* receive. This becomes something of a double-edged sword: while the obsession turns to the self, the person's self-worth relies on the validation of others. To shift out of this mindset, teens need an outlet for interacting with others in a way that is mutually beneficial.

The whole purpose of the "Link Up" movement is to build up others while building up yourself. Socially at-risk children need a stable, consistent, one-on-one interaction with another person. When children feel confident and secure, they're more likely to succeed in school and achieve personal goals. Meanwhile, mentors can gain self-esteem and sense of purpose from helping their mentee.

People who volunteer their time, donate to a favorite charity, or aid someone in need of attention, have higher self-esteem and overall well-being. Helping socially at-risk children means you are vulnerable to their needs and your own emotions, which drives connection and fosters a deeper sense of purpose. By shifting your thinking from things all about yourself and toward helping others while doing something that matters to you, your self-esteem, sense of purpose, and feelings of connection increase dramatically.

Takeaways for Teachers:

- Social media has many beneficial uses, but needs to be used in moderation.
- Teens who use too much social media can become addicted to the dopamine fix of receiving "likes" and positive feedback.
- When most interactions need to happen online due to a health crisis like COVID-19, you should prioritize synchronous conversations on clients like Zoom or Skype rather than asynchronous social media platforms that rely on likes and comments.
- If teens cut back on social media, they may have more time to spend in an activity that prioritizes face-to-face connection, like a mentorship program.

NOTES

1. Ruder, Debra Bradley. "Screen Time and the Brain." *Harvard Medical School*, 19 June 2019. https://hms.harvard.edu/news/screen-time-brain

2. Hawkey, Elizabeth. "Media use in childhood: Evidence-based recommendations for caregivers." *American Psychological Association*, May 2019. https://www.apa.org/pi/families/resources/newsletter/2019/05/media-use-childhood

Chapter 4

Starting the Day off Right

The dreaded alarm sounds and the day begins. Wiping your eyes, you get out of bed hoping to make the most of your day. Setting the tone for a good day, for many, is about how you look when you walk out the door. High school aged students are no different, but sleeping an extra 15 minutes can be too tempting. Late nights spent dealing with family or friend conflicts—or just spent on Snapchat, TikTok, Instagram, or YouTube—makes for a restless night for a lot of teenagers.

Sometimes, comfort and timeliness dictate how you look when you walk out the door. Look good, feel good, right? As far back as 2016, the Link Up program was looking to help children feel good about themselves. Feeling good about yourself builds self-esteem and makes for a better day and life. Many children suffer from low self-esteem and it starts at a young age.

HYGIENE AND SELF-ESTEEM

Basic hygiene is an important part of building self-esteem.[1] Bathing, brushing your hair, brushing your teeth, trimming your nails, and others makes everyone feel better. A person's grooming conveys contentiousness, which earns respect. A child who feels good about their appearance will be more confident, which will lead to an easier time making friends. A child who comes to school dirty and unkempt may find that other children are reluctant to sit by them, or they may even be bullied.

Poor hygiene is often indicative of a larger problem in the child's life. Some families do not have the resources to provide proper hygiene. Some children are just too young to totally provide their own personal care, but their family members are too busy or unable to assist. Some children have not been taught personal hygiene. For some children, poor hygiene may be a sign of depression. Poor hygiene should always be investigated to evaluate the need for intervention from social services.

THE SCHOOL SALON

Setting your alarm to go off 45 minutes early, twice a week, for no other reason than to help a child is quite a selfless act for a teenager. This was the case for seven senior girls in 2016. The Link Up program was in its first year at Meredosia-Chambersburg. These girls, in many ways, set the tone for everything that has happened since then. As is mentioned throughout the book, many of the children that come through the school doors are impoverished and lack a positive feeling about themselves.

Back in 2016, the Link Up program met twice a week on Tuesdays and Thursdays—currently, the program meets on every weekday morning, five days a week. Building up a child's self-esteem in a short period of time, two days a week, took some thinking outside the box. With the primary focus being on girls from first grade through third grade, the seven high school seniors decided to set up a salon in one of the classrooms.

Looking nice and feeling good about yourself promotes a positive self-image. Wanting to offer a positive self-image to everyone who wanted to participate, these girls made the salon available to anyone who wanted to sign up.

Setting up their first salon, located inside the first grade classroom, took a little planning. With the school's administration on board, and all parents notified, it was time to get started. For safety purposes, no hair supplies could be shared, so the mentors created an individual "beauty bag" for each girl in first through third grade. The bags included brushes, ribbons, hair ties, scrunchies, and brightly colored bows. Not all girls participated, but it was important for all to feel welcome. The seven senior girls arrived at 7:30 to set up shop, ready for anyone who needed some special attention.

Whenever a child would arrive, they would be met by a smiling and gracious high school senior. Each primary school girl entered with some apprehension, but that was soon replaced with a confident smile. The senior hair stylist would sit them down and ask, "What would you like done today?" Many of the kids didn't know what hair options they had, so the senior girls offered some suggestions, including a simple ponytail, a double French-braid, braided bangs, a bun or top knot, or a side pony. It's a good thing the senior girls were there, because the teacher in charge was bald and didn't have a clue there were that many options.

As the days passed and everyone could see how neat and happy each child felt, more and more girls wanted the special attention. Each week, more students wanted to sign up for the before-school salon. Soon, the line was forming and was stretching out into the hallway. A child would enter feeling a little "frumpy" and leave feeling loved and pretty.

CONFIDENCE IS BEAUTIFUL

Children need the opportunity to feel good about themselves. It is human nature to compare yourself to someone else. When children feel like they measure up to their peers, it builds their body image. According to psychologist D'Arcy Lyness, "A healthy body image comes from accepting your body, liking it, and taking care of it. Even when there are things kids can't do, they can feel good about what they can do."[2] Even more important than the special hair styles was the time the child was able to spend with the high school student.

One-on-one time with a child is very beneficial to a child's self-esteem. It conveys the message that they are important and that they matter. When they feel valued by someone else, their own self-value improves. One-on-one time provides an opportunity to practice communication skills. Children learn how to relate to others. The child can openly express themselves without being judged by groups of peers. This interaction teaches them about sharing and kindness. These positive behaviors will be important as they build relationships throughout their lifetime.

Walking the hallways at Meredosia-Chambersburg, you will find multiple banners with positive sayings on them to provide motivation and perspective. One of the banners added to the collection was one that defined selflessness. Since 2014, the Meredosia-Chambersburg School District has been placing an emphasis on selfless acts by incorporating the Link Up program for teenagers.

The banner reads: *Being selfless is a mindset. On a simple level, it's about putting someone else before you. It's about doing somebody a favor even when it hurts you a little. It's about realizing that life isn't just about your needs and preferences, but rather looking out for another's, as well.*

Teaching high school kids about the need to be selfless is overdue. Showing them the way with concrete examples and opportunities is the first step. The following sections of this book will provide concrete examples of how the Link Up program has worked, how to build a solid foundation, and how to instill selfless qualities in mentors and mentees alike.

When the Link Up program opened up a salon on the elementary end of the building, senior girls developed their own sense of what selflessness meant. Getting up early was not as painful when you felt the satisfaction of a job well done. The Link Up program will forever be indebted to the seven senior girls for their selfless acts.

Takeaways for Teachers:

- Self-confidence presents itself in a variety of ways, including a child's personal hygiene and outward appearance.
- When children struggle with hygiene or positive body image, a larger problem in that child's home life is likely present.
- Sometimes, improving a child's self-esteem requires some creative thinking outside the box, like the seven high school seniors did when creating a school hair salon.

NOTES

1. Burton, Neel. "Building Confidence and Self-Esteem." *Psychology Today*. 30 May 2012. https://www.psychologytoday.com/us/blog/hide-and-seek/201205/building-confidence-and-self-esteem

2. Lyness, D'Arcy. "Encouraging a Healthy Body Image." *KidsHealth*, 2018. https://kidshealth.org/en/parents/body-image.html

Section 2

FOUNDATIONS OF A MENTORSHIP PROGRAM

Chapter 5

Identifying Socially At-Risk Children

Socially at-risk children share common characteristics from an early age, which tend to become obvious around kindergarten. For the first time, kids are put into social situations with peers that reveal similar characteristics. Characteristics of socially at-risk children, which are fairly consistent from child to child, tend to include the inability to effectively communicate thoughts and feelings, struggles to socialize with other kids, and difficulties keeping up with schoolwork.

These children tend to take one of two paths. Some socially at-risk children already have a level of confidence and strong self-esteem, and do not desire to make friends. Other children strive to fit in, and when it doesn't come naturally to them because of their differences, the result is being isolated and ignored. In both cases, the children end up with a sense of loneliness. This isolation means socially at-risk children miss opportunities to socialize

Gaining skills for communication, sharing, and listening at an early age is critical to overall social development—without opportunities to socialize and build these skills, the child will fall behind socially. Much of this experience plays out on the playground during recess. The children who miss out in this area can eventually become anti-social, which results in a feeling of invisibility. Feeling invisible at home and now feeling invisible at school causes withdrawal and envy. From this point on, the cycle continues, and the child's chances for social acceptance are limited.

WHERE DOES THE CHILD CALL HOME?

A child's environment plays a pivotal role in their development. Many of the environmental factors influencing early child development involve the physical surroundings in and around their home. Where the child calls home is an early indicator for future success.

Shelter is a basic human need, along with food and water; when these needs aren't fulfilled, a child cannot focus on succeeding in school or making friends. A child whose home is filthy or dangerous, or a child who lacks a consistent home whatsoever, is going to struggle with fitting in at school. A well-nurtured child does better than a deprived one; the child's environment contributes to this.

A good school and a loving family build in children strong social and interpersonal skills, which will enable them to excel in other areas such as academics and extra-curricular events. The child raised in a stressful environment with poor role models will not have the same experience. Many of the social aspects that encompass a child's day-to-day life will dictate early development.

UNSTABLE FAMILY LIFE

Families have the most profound impact in nurturing a child and determining the ways in which they develop psychologically and socially. Whether they are raised by their parents, grandparents, or in foster care, children need basic love, care, and courtesy to develop as healthy, functioning individuals.

The most positive growth occurs when families invest time, energy, and love in the development of the child through activities, such as family reading time, family game night, or simply having heartfelt conversations.

Children long for and thrive in stable home environments. Stability provides structure, consistency, and strength that support the child emotionally and psychologically.[1] When a child's family environment changes due to financial difficulties, divorce, or remarriage, the parent's mental health or ability to parent may suffer, which can lead to behavioral difficulties for the child as well.

Instability can also lead to learning difficulties, as children may struggle to concentrate when they are worried about situations they cannot control. Many children suffer from attachment disruptions when their parents frequently bring different partners into their children's lives. Sleeping in different homes, moving to new schools, and having constantly changing stepsiblings all bring a lack of stability.

Families that abuse or neglect children affect their positive development. These children, in large numbers, will end up with poor social skills and difficulty bonding with other people as adults. Jennifer Shore, Executive Director of Focus for Health, defines childhood trauma as "an event that a child finds overwhelmingly distressing or emotionally painful often resulting in lasting mental or physical effects."[2] The effects of childhood trauma can have lasting impacts on a child's well-being, such as:

- Affecting their perception of reality
- Wiring their brain to expect danger
- Triggering fight, flight, or freeze responses
- Increasing stress hormones flowing through the body
- Creating relationship and behavioral problems
- Taking away a sense of safety
- Creating a sense of hopelessness[3]

The brains and bodies of children grow differently when living in situations perceived to be unsafe or neglectful. Nurturing and affection during difficult times can help mitigate the developmental problems that may ensue. Stability is paramount for a child to succeed. If they do not experience it at home, it becomes even more important for them to experience it at school.

HOW ENVIRONMENT IMPACTS EDUCATION

A child doesn't get to pick their family or where they are raised. Where a child lives has a great influence on how the child turns out, socially. The school they attend, the neighborhood they live in, and the opportunities offered by the community and their peer circles are some of the social factors affecting a child's development.

Living in an enriching community that has parks, libraries, and community centers for group activities and sports all play a role in developing the child's skills, talents, and behavior. Uninteresting communities can and will push many children not to go outside often, but instead to play video games and lose themselves in social media inside. The climate in and around a child's home will dictate their ability to learn socially acceptable behaviors.

Money and social status will matter when a child is developing social awareness. The socio-economic status of a family determines the quality of the opportunity a child gets. Wealthy families can offer better learning resources for their children and they can afford special aid if their children need it. Children from poorer families may not have access to educational resources and good nutrition to reach their full potential. They may also have working parents who work too many hours and cannot invest enough quality time in their development.

Learning involves much more than the academic portion of traditional schooling. A child's education should build them up mentally, intellectually, emotionally, and socially so they operate as healthy, functioning members of society. School is where the development of the mind takes place and the child can gain some maturity.

Reinforcement is a component of learning where an activity or exercise is repeated and refined to solidify the lessons learned. Any lesson worth learning must be repeated until the right results are obtained. Many socially at-risk children learn lessons again and again, but they are often the kind of lesson they should forget—for example, they might learn that food is scarce or that their parents are unreliable.

This lack of nurturing on a young child will impact their life forever. The socially at-risk child struggles to form deep and lasting relationships and lacks fundamentally strong trust in humanity.

THE IMPORTANCE OF LEARNING EMPATHY

Young children naturally have a playful and curious spirit about them. Teachers often enjoy sitting back and watching their young students innocently explore the world around them. The child that is not properly attended to, treasured, and loved often loses this childlike spirit. Without intervention, it can be damaged for good. Many times, children stricken with poor parenting are given the blame and often feel the shame. The child will eventually stop trying, and the loneliness that follows may actually be easier to deal with than the shame, humiliation, or neglect. Ignoring or neglecting a child's needs can create many symptoms and ultimately mental health problems, which will affect all areas of their life.

The importance of learning empathy applies here as well. How can a child grow up knowing how to provide empathy and nurturing if they have never experienced it? When children are loved and treated well, they don't grow up wanting to hurt others; they grow up wanting to help and respect others, and they develop the ability to provide empathy.

Teaching children empathy is critical for helping them build healthy relationships. The essential way for a child to integrate empathy is for the child to experience it. Often, a caring teacher may want to fix the child's problem for them. That is not always possible, and it takes away the child's self-efficacy. According to psychotherapist Erin Leonard, "honoring and resonating with a child's feeling state is what helps them, not rescuing them from their problem."[4] You cannot save a child from feeling hurt, angry, disappointed, or sad. You can make them feel acknowledged and understood.

Take a minute and recall how it feels when someone truly believes in you and validates your feelings. Empathy is the greatest gift to give a socially at-risk child. Almost every classroom in the world has a child that comes from a dysfunctional home where showing empathy has never been a priority. Teachers that oversee their room of children can see through observation who these children are.

Teachers are overwhelmed with too many kids, behavior issues, and learning problems. Trying to fix all of them at one time is endless and exhausting. Many times, the child that lacks empathy is capable of learning, but needs to be taught. They can learn to love and trust, but they must feel love and trust first.

SPREADING EMPATHY THROUGH MENTORING

The Link Up Mentoring Program was designed to identify and assist the very children that are socially at-risk. As mentioned above, no one knows the child quite like the teacher in charge of their care. The teacher is privy to information, observation, and the full picture of each child's needs. The teacher, in need of help themselves, is grateful for the extra hand when a mentor comes to work with one of their at-risk children.

Millions of students throughout the world that have learned to love, because they were loved, and are ready and able to love the identified child. The cooperating school identifies the high school mentor, the teacher identifies the child, and the internship provides the guidelines to implement. The high school mentor is under the guidance of the teacher in charge and the child will learn from the two.

Every child deserves a chance in life. They didn't pick their parents, their neighborhood, or their community, but as an educator, you can pick a caring person to share part of their day with them. Schools can and should be a place of love, trust and respect for every child.

Takeaways for Teachers:

- Socially at-risk children are those who struggle with communication, social interaction, and problem-solving with peers. They may lack stability at home or lack a caregiver who models acceptable behavior for them.

- Many social at-risk children deal with other issues at home, including food scarcity, rotating caregivers, or financial trouble.
- Because their basic needs aren't always met, many socially at-risk children are unable to focus on learning in the classroom and developing friendships.
- Socially at-risk children need to be shown empathy so they can learn how to later show empathy for others.
- A dedicated one-on-one mentor can be a great way for a socially at-risk child to learn empathy and practice developing a social bond.

NOTES

1. Hatter, Kathryn, (2017) https://howtoadult.com/lack-stability-affects-children-13458.html

2. Shore, Jennifer (2020)https://www.focusforhealth.org/the-relationship-between-trauma-and-resiliency-in-children/

3. Ibid.

4. Leonard, Erin. "The Secret to Teaching a Child Empathy." *Psychology Today*. 16 December 2018. https://www.psychologytoday.com/us/blog/peaceful-parenting/201812/the-secret-teaching-child-empathy

Chapter 6

Laying Foundations through Relationships

At the end of every summer, children gather for their first day of a new school year. Nervous the night before, unable to sleep, anxious to meet their new friends, many children wonder, "Will I like my new teacher? Will they be mean or nice? Will I be in class with my best friends from last year?"

The school building is the place where the academic and social life of most children begins. Children learn such a vast array of knowledge, from how things around them work, to the similarities and differences they have with their classmates, to the importance of speaking up and forming their own opinions.

As children grow up, their ability to form and sustain relationships with classmates and teachers is critical. Many children will naturally acquire these skills as they develop; however, other children may, for various reasons, need some help with building relationships. If all children and young people are able to form and maintain positive relationships in ways that make sense to them, then their social development will be off to a strong start.

When a child experiences adversity early in life, stressors may develop that stay present as they get older. Much of this stress has long-term negative consequences for physical and emotional well-being, educational outcomes, interpersonal relationships, and overall comfort.

Moreover, responsive relationships early in life are the most important factors in laying a strong foundation of mental awareness.

Educators encourage responsive relationships for all elementary children under their care. Teachers and staff have the task of promoting responsive caregiving and modeling how to respond positively to young elementary children.

Responsive teaching involves stepping out of a learning activity to support the student's needs at that given time—in other words, responding to a student's needs as they come, even if that means adjusting the plans for the day. This approach allows for conversation and play that promotes interactions between adults and children. Responsive teaching has become more difficult due to the seemingly constant need of some students.

When you look back on your favorite teachers from childhood, who sticks out in your mind? Normally, adults have the fondest memories of teachers who made class fun, who engaged them in interactive learning, and who made them feel important. When you look back on the teachers you dreaded, what were they like? Many people would say that their worst memories of school came from teachers who placed discipline above communication, who lectured about difficult material instead of letting students ask questions, or who were just boring!

When you enjoy teaching, making the class fun comes more naturally; however, this idealistic view of teaching isn't sustainable all the time. The reality is, making every student feel special every day can be a challenge, especially when multiple students require specialized one-on-one assistance. Some teachers have 30 students in their classroom and no aide. Some teachers have 10 different students who need extra attention at the exact same time. Sometimes, you can't do it alone.

Link Up mentors can bridge this gap by giving students extra attention outside of the classroom. Socially at-risk-students don't always need extra assistance academically, but they do need someone to give them extra emotional attention and make them feel special. Responsive teaching for the entire class becomes easier when you have assistance meeting the needs of the socially at-risk student. In this way, the Link Up mentor helps the entire classroom, not just the student they are individually mentoring.

BUILDING STRONG RELATIONSHIPS, ONE MENTOR AT A TIME

Children who have mentors experience a multitude of benefits both while in the mentoring relationship and after it ends. Elementary children who build relationships with mentors learn how to set healthy boundaries and create connections with others. By spending time with a high school aged student outside of their families, they improve their communication and interpersonal skills, which helps the child build stronger relationships with their family members, friends, and teachers. These skills will continue growing throughout adulthood.

Constantly fighting low self-esteem and instability in their home life leaves the child with little room to advance in relationship building. A good mentoring relationship can help the child see themselves accurately and recognize their strengths and accomplishments. Socially at-risk children who live in underserved communities or who don't have a stable adult relationship in their lives often struggle with their behavior in school and at home. Having a mentor helps them learn how to control themselves and behave properly in a wide variety of settings, especially school.

There are thousands of stories where mentors have stabilized and enhanced the life of a troubled child. Sadly, the number of children needing mentoring is reaching alarming numbers.

Shortly after starting the Link Up program at Meredosia-Chambersburg, a grandmother called the school distraught and searching for help. She was also brutally honest: during the course of the phone call she described how her daughter would frequently change boyfriends and live at different places throughout the school year. Her grandson, falling behind in school, never knew for sure where he would lay his head down to sleep. The lack of stability in the boy's life kept him withdrawn socially.

The school immediately Linked Up the young boy with a high school mentor. A strong and trusting relationship developed. Meeting up before class with his new friend became a constant in this boy's life, providing him with a much-needed sense of stability. For the first time, the young boy was looking forward to school, the one place he knew he had a stable and consistent routine. The grandmother was thankful and eagerly shared her grandson's success with her friends. Soon after, the program was receiving calls for action from other parents and grandparents.

One of the calls came from a mother whose daughter continually contracted head lice and was constantly made fun of by classmates. The problem grew so out of hand that the eight-year-old girl was refusing to go to school and would cry every morning. With no answers of her own, the mother called the school looking for help. The Link Up program was ready and willing to step in.

Consulting with other teachers and administration, the program chose to Link Up this student with a high school senior. This senior, the school's Homecoming Queen, was the perfect choice for two reasons: first, the girl was popular and all the girls in the elementary school wanted to be her friend. Secondly, and most important, she had the same problem when she was eight. Yes, the Homecoming Queen had head lice in second grade and was also teased.

After sharing her story and meeting up every day with the affected child, everything calmed down, and the little girl was happy and eager to go to school. Relationship building in the middle of chaos is forever gratifying.

More than likely, this eight-year-old girl will remember the ridicule she felt throughout her life, but it will sting less because of the intervention of the Link Up program. Without the intervention, this situation could have had an enormous impact on her life. She could have missed out on valuable education; her self-esteem could have continued to plummet. She could have become extremely introverted and avoided all relationships as a self-protection mechanism to avoid pain. Even worse, she could have become a bully herself, inflicting harm to try to make herself feel better.

Instead, she will have a great memory of how someone wanted to be her friend. She will remember that a case of head lice isn't an insurmountable problem; after all, her *role model* overcame the exact same thing! She learned kindness, how to receive it and how to give it: a lesson that has the potential to change many lives as she grows and matures into adulthood.

TALK FIRST, THEN TAKE ACTION

Stories like this—at times, even worse—are often discussed among teachers, but too often the discussion ends with talk. Talking about your problems within a classroom, with your colleagues, or with a specific child helps alleviate some of the stress and that's important, but it doesn't create an actionable solution for the child.

Still developing, most children are not yet emotionally equipped to deal with the interpersonal conflict that arises from ridicule. Children are likely to experience anxiety and their self-esteem will continue to spiral downward.

Building relationships is the cornerstone of child development. Socially at-risk children or children simply hitting a rough patch in life have untapped potential being held back due to poor relationships in and out of school.

Takeaways for Teachers:

- The most powerful relationships with students are responsive ones.
- A one-on-one mentorship can provide students with a responsive relationship *outside* the classroom, which sets them up for success *inside* the classroom.
- As kids are developing emotionally, communication is one of the most powerful skills to develop.
- Older mentors can serve as role models to help children deal with day-to-day interpersonal conflicts outside of the classroom, such as bullying.
- Talking about an at-risk child with your colleagues, or with the child themselves, is only useful if followed up with an actionable plan to help, such as finding the student a mentor.

Chapter 7

Building Momentum by Building Self-Esteem

Every morning a child wakes up can be a reminder of a life that is unforgiving. Without the right resources at their disposal, and not yet old enough to seek out those resources for themselves, children can easily become discouraged and need your help to build momentum. Safety guides on airplanes will remind you that, in the case of an emergency, you should secure our own oxygen masks and life vests before helping a child with theirs; as an adult, you have to build momentum and self-esteem in your own life before a child can rely on you.

Building momentum in life requires removing things that frequently hold you back and replacing them with things that move you forward. Sounds simple, right? Momentum, by definition, requires consistent push in the right direction to keep things rolling. To overcome the occasional bump in the road, you use momentum to keep moving toward a positive result.

There come many situations in life which you can classify as difficult. A wise thing to do is to be prepared to face the difficult times in your life. These events usually affect you deeply on a psychological level and could potentially damage your life. Proper preparation for these times could help you to improve how you live your life. All this preparation allows you to face the challenges to learn and grow. Making the best of everything life throws at you is sometimes enough.

BUILDING MOMENTUM AS AN ADULT

Imagine the following scenario: you've spent 10 years in the relationship of your dreams with a spouse you love. You have two wonderful children together, and life feels great. Then, one day, your partner reveals that they no longer want to be married. Within a few months, you're in the middle of a rough divorce, including meetings with lawyers and shared custody of beloved children. This situation would likely take a huge toll on your self-esteem. You might feel turbulence taking over your forward momentum, your traction slipping, and ultimately progress toward your career goals halting.

In this situation, because you are an adult, you would likely have access to resources to help you rebuild your momentum. For example, you might have health insurance or some money in savings that allows you to see a therapist. Maybe you have the ability to move to a new neighborhood for a change of scenery. Maybe your job offers the flexibility to let you take some time off, or maybe you're in a position to choose a new career. Regardless of circumstances, because you're an adult, you have the knowledge of what resources are available to you and the life experience to know which ones to employ.

Adults feel a similar loss of momentum when failing to achieve a major goal. While everyone views failure differently, and while some embrace it more than others, failure tends to create a feeling of worthlessness. As an adult, you also have resources to help you rebuild your momentum after failure, whether it's through the support of colleagues or through internet access to educate yourself further.

Now, imagine this scenario: just months after your divorce, you find yourself dealing with your father's death. Death of a loved one, one of life's greatest challenges, can happen at anytime to anyone, casting a shadow of sorrow on everything in your life. In this case, you might become angry, yearning for closure. You might become depressed, struggling to adapt to your daily routine without that important person in your life. You need to return to work as a teacher; you have students counting on you. But how can you be there for your students when you're dealing with so much trauma yourself?

Identifying your resources is crucial, whether it's family members you can rely on for emotional strength, a therapist you can visit if your mental health struggles, or a savings account to serve as a financial safety net. When you're in a situation that threatens your own momentum and self-esteem, a struggling student might slip past your radar. Once you've built your own momentum, it's time to be that resource to help your students do the same.

Children often face many of the same struggles building momentum and self-esteem that adults do, but they are more likely to lack the resources to help themselves and the emotional intelligence to know how to use them.

A child with no access to their parent's health insurance card can't easily see a therapist on their own; never mind that many have no car to drive to get there. Even when children do seek out resources to cope with difficulties, they often lack the experience to use them responsibly; for example, a teenager suffering from family trauma might turn to drugs to self-medicate rather than seeking professional help.

A lack of resources, combined with a lack of control over life circumstances, can leave a child without a chance to build momentum and destroy their feeling of self-worth. Children with low self-esteem find it hard to cope when they make a mistake, lose, or fail. The result is an inability to reach their full potential. Recognizing and addressing the needs of children with low self-esteem is necessary to prepare them for success.

HOW CHILDREN BUILD SELF-ESTEEM

The American Academy of Pediatrics[1] suggests that a child develops self-esteem based in part on the expectations of important people in their life, such as parents and teachers, and how close that child's self-image reflects the vision of others. Before a child can achieve a sense of self-esteem, that child must first gain a sense of responsibility and control over their own circumstances as well as a network of adults and peers that they can trust.

Children also need the right tools to handle failure when it does happen. As a teacher, you have the power to offer your students constructive feedback that both points out their strengths and identifies areas of improvement. The American Academy of Pediatrics explains that supportive feedback helps students overcome feelings of failure, along with the shame and guilt that might accompany it. Everyone, regardless of age, needs to hear words of encouragement; but for children, who might be experiencing an insurmountable problem for the first time in their lives, need to know they have a support network ready to cheer them on toward their goals.

HOW TEACHERS AND MENTORS CAN HELP

Teachers at every grade level across the country are aware of their students' obstacles and try to help. Many times, the teacher successfully builds momentum in a child and rebuilds their self-worth. But, for as many that have success, there are that many that fail to connect. Finding a solution to the children that cannot be helped within a traditional school setting is the primary reason for the Link Up Program. Children that live and deal with chaos their whole life and feel nothing but failure deserve a chance to succeed in life.

One of the students in the Link Up Program was dealing with a lack of self-esteem due to circumstances at home; while his story is devastating at first, it also illustrates how adults can help rebuild that sense of self-worth.

Picture a traditional third-grade classroom with 16 students with one teacher and a classroom aide. One morning, the kids were engaged in a language lesson when one child screamed, "Mouse!"

A mouse was skittering across the classroom floor. In typical third-grade fashion, kids scattered throughout the room, and chaos ensued.

For being such a little creature, the mouse is mighty when it comes to mayhem. How did the mouse get in the room and where did it come from?

The answer to the question came in the form of a backpack. The teacher had noticed a smell coming from a certain place in the room and decided to check it out. When the students were at lunch, the teacher and custodial staff began a search for the unpleasant smell. They narrowed it down to a backpack that belonged to one little boy in the class. Inside the backpack, to their nauseating dismay, they found a live mouse and three dead mice inside the boy's backpack. The mouse running free came from the bag and the child's home.

The child became embarrassed and self-conscious when the teacher discussed the mouse with him. Most likely, he didn't like the new vision his teacher had of his home environment. Soon, this student became distracted and began failing his classes. Though he visited a social worker for 15 minutes once a week, the limited time together left the child without a lasting impact.

Noticing the boy's decreased self-esteem, his teacher sought the advice of the Link Up Program, imagining the boy could benefit from a mentor. That boy was paired up with a high-school varsity basketball player as his mentor. As the third-grade boy got to know his new high-school senior mentor, he began to look forward to arriving at school each morning, where he'd get to see his new friend and role model.

Despite the challenges of building momentum for this child, he began to heal. Soon, his smile returned in the classroom and his grades began to improve. Other kids in his class were jealous of his friendship with a cool, older basketball player. While the cleanliness of his home was still outside of his control, he had developed a sense of self-worth at school. There are so many boys and girls with similar households as this little boy, but there are also just as many high-school boys and girls to step in and provide selfless service to those in need.

The difference between a child and an adult in developing and maintaining self-esteem is the ability to care for oneself. A child lacks the life experience and emotional maturity to figure out their worth when surrounded by nothing but negativity. Identify the child or children in need of care. Link Up, build momentum, build self-esteem, and give the child hope. Every school in America has the resources to help build momentum and self-esteem. Those resources are the people who are willing to give a hand and make a difference.

Takeaways for Teachers:

- Make sure you've built a positive momentum in your own life, and then serve as a role model for your students.
- Identify the similarities and differences in the ways that adults and children build self-esteem.
- Remember that your expectations and feedback will influence a child's self-esteem, for better or worse.

NOTE

1. https://www.healthychildren.org/English/ages-stages/gradeschool/Pages/Helping-Your-Child-Develop-A-Healthy-Sense-of-Self-Esteem.aspx

.

Chapter 8

Link Up and Own It

"Owning it" is what the high school students at Meredosia-Chambersburg, the birthplace of the Link Up Program, call keeping a promise. When they Link Up with their younger mentees, they "own it"; that means they keep the promises they made to that child, even when it's inconvenient.

A promise is a verbal agreement to one's self or to others—a commitment with the implied intention to follow through no matter what. Keeping promises shows that a person is honest. When a person keeps a promise, they demonstrate trustworthiness and reliability. A kept promise brings security to a relationship. In business transactions, kept promises reflect credibility. For personal relationships, keeping promises promotes trust. For a young child still learning about trust, a broken promise can be devastating.

PERSUASIVE PROMISES IN PARENTING

Building trust in any relationship is the first step in a healthy and long-lasting life together. Often parents might make a *persuasive promise*: a commitment to a certain outcome based on their child's behavior. When parents break a promise, they are unintentionally teaching their children not to trust them. If a parent promises their child a reward for accomplishing a certain goal, and then doesn't follow through once the child completes their end of the bargain, the child loses trust for their parent.

When a parent promises their child something, they are assuring the child that they are a priority. If that parent breaks the promise, the child receives the message that they're less important. Broken promises can have a cumulative effect of lowering a child's self-esteem.

Another example of a persuasive promise is when a parent makes unrealistic empty threats when a child disobeys. Often these threats are made in the heat of the moment when a parent is mad or distraught. A parent might threaten to ground a child for a month for neglecting to clean their room, and then later, when the heat of the moment has passed, decide not to follow through. Often these threats have no lasting impact after the parent's frustration has passed. Children soon learn that overpromises, whether for rewards or punishments, have no lasting impact.[1]

HOW BROKEN PROMISES IMPACT CHILDREN

When parents divorce, they might make promises to ease their child's pain. Divorce occurs in homes at a high frequency and often the children are adversely affected. During a divorce, children often struggle with unanswered questions and emotions that are difficult for them to verbalize. Their parents have broken a promise to one another and the trust they had in each of them is compromised. Some families make the best of a shared custody situation, and the children receive love and respect in both homes. However, this is not the case in all divorces.

One of the more common broken promises when parents divorce is the failure to show up for visitations, which gives the child false hope. If it routinely happens, the child may have a hard time recovering lost trust. Another very common and traumatic broken promise is when parents say something like, "We are trying to work things out so we can be a family again." This promise is used to heal for the moment and has the best intention, but it is destructive from a trust standpoint. When the family doesn't reconcile then the words that were used for healing become hollow.

Many people say that children are like sponges. They soak up everything around them. If they are surrounded by inconsistencies and broken promises, they will expect this as the norm. They will soon accept dishonesty as acceptable behavior and will replicate the learned behavior.

A parent is a role model. If the parent does not keep their word, what motivation does the child have to keep theirs? The child may require a powerful influence from a consistent, honest, and reliable connection in their life to rebuild that trust.

Every person needs to break promises sometimes; unforeseen circumstances can lead to inevitable changes in plans. What matters is how that person responds to their own broken promise. When a person admits their mistake and explains honestly why the mistake happened, it can go a long way in repairing the damage that was made to the trust.

EMPHASIZING PROMISES IN MENTORSHIP

Building a trusting and lasting relationship takes time. It takes commitment, discipline, and timeliness. The most important aspect of the Link Up program is the consistent, disciplined approach of showing up every day. Many of the children that are identified as socially at-risk live with broken promises from their own families.

Showing up on time with a caring attitude, every day that school is in session, will go a long way in developing trust. Listening becomes the next most important component to building trust. In a world with everyone's nose in a phone or computer screen, its refreshing to have undivided attention with someone listening to your every word. Communication is primary in developing trust. With your attention on the identified child growing with each day, you find the child building in self-esteem and trust.

The Link Up mentor learns the importance of a timely commitment. They will see the child grow in confidence, and they will feel the trust and respect the child will have for them. This can be an amazing and empowering moment for the mentor. The impact is two-fold: the mentor and the mentee are equally rewarded with the comfort of trust.

Listening and sharing without condemning is crucial in building faith. By allowing the identified child to have some say in the relationship and allowing them to share without fear of being judged, the mentor can set a tone for a successful time together. The identified child wants to share their thoughts and experiences even though at first, they may seem reluctant. When the two have spent quality and disciplined time together, they have proven to each other a sense of dependability.

Link Up mentors promise their mentee that they'll see them every morning. They promise that child undivided attention. And when they make a promise, they own it!

Takeaways for Teachers:

- Children learn trust from their parents; not all parents set a good example.
- To build a successful mentorship with a child, mentors need to show repeat and consistent efforts to keep promises.
- When you need to break a promise to a child, explain the reasons behind the decision, the circumstances that led to it. Apologize and take accountability for your mistake.

NOTE

1. Pickhardt, C. Adolescence and the Power of Promises. 2018. https ://www.pspychologytoday.com/us/blog/surviving-your-childs-adolescence/ 201810/adolescence-and-the-power-promises

Chapter 9

The Importance of Caregiver Involvement

You can't go outside and play until your schoolwork is done. No electronics until you read for 30 minutes. Sound familiar? Maybe that's something you say to your kids, or maybe it's something you remember dreading when your parents said it to you.

Emphasizing the importance of education is every caregiver's responsibility, but for some parents or guardians, it's not a priority. According to the *International Journal of Human Behavior*, the one of the best predictors of student success is the extent to which families encourage learning at home and involve themselves in their child's education.[1] When parents are engaged in their children's school lives, students have the home support and knowledge they need to not only finish the assigned work, but also develop a lifelong love of learning.

In addition to parents, children have many types of caregivers and guardians. Business Wire reports that 2.7 million grandparents are serving as guardians for their grandchildren.[2] These grandparents are raising 2 percent of the children in the United States. While 2 percent may not sound significant, that number represents 2.9 million children. The Child Trends Databank reports that in 2017, approximately 443,000 children lived in foster homes. Of those 443,000 children, 45 percent of them lived in nonrelative homes.[3]

While grandparents and foster parents want to see the children in their care succeed, these children are not living with their parents for a reason. Usually the reason involves trauma for the child, such as parental drug abuse, incarcerated parents, physical or sexual abuse, or neglect. For these children, stumbling blocks are already in place. The importance of their caregiver being involved in their education is even more important.

WHY SHOULD CAREGIVERS GET INVOLVED?

Teachers that focus on guardian engagement often see a profound change in their classrooms. When the child knows that their teacher and caregiver are working together, it makes the work for both a lot easier. The more parents engage in their children's education, the better for all students in the class; when a few students' behavior and engagement improves, the effect can be contagious to the others. Encouraging parent and guardian engagement is more than common courtesy; it's a necessity.

Although, as mentioned above, there can be many types of caregivers, the remainder of this chapter will refer to "parents" for the sake of conciseness. Feel free to substitute the word "parent" with "grandparent," "guardian," "caregiver," or any other terms that may apply to the specific student in question.

Parent engagement places academic performance in the hands of both parent and teacher. When parents help their kids with homework assignments, giving them positive daily feedback on their strengths and constructive criticism on their weaknesses, students learn teamwork. When parents talk to their kids outside of school about the projects they're doing and subject matter they're learning, students remember that education spans beyond the classroom.

Parent engagement happens when teachers involve the parents in school meetings or events, or when parents volunteer their support at home and school. The child sees the commitment between their parents and teacher, which is a good model for how to make a commitment to their own schoolwork. Parents prioritizing educational goals promote an effective learning environment.

Parental involvement refers to the amount a parent participates in their child's school life. Some schools and teachers foster healthy parental involvement through events and volunteer opportunities, but sometimes it's up to the parents to involve themselves in their child's education. Parents can ensure that their child receives the benefits from parental involvement by staying up to date on what is happening in the classroom and knowing events on the school calendar. Parental involvement does not guarantee school success, but history tells you it is the single best indicator of student success. Many times, children that are blessed with parental involvement are more likely to enroll in higher-level programs, pass their classes, attend school regularly, have better social skills, and move onto post-secondary education.

WHAT HOLDS PARENTS BACK?

Parental involvement is important, but a large portion of parents neglect this important role. Why would a parent neglect this golden chance to enhance learning? There are many reasons for this. Most parents have to work to maintain a financial standing for the family, and some work long hours during the day and the night, leaving them without much time to get involved at school.

Some parents don't feel welcome at the school. They might have had a bad school experience and don't care to relive it, such as poor grades or discipline issues that bring back traumatic feelings. Some parents feel inadequate from an intellectual standpoint and want nothing to do with the inside of a school building. A parent that lacks a clear understanding of the benefits of school and the importance of their involvement keeps them away. By not knowing or understanding the importance of working together, parents might blame the school or the teacher instead of taking accountability for the child's failure.

HOW CAN TEACHERS HELP?

When parents are unable to take part in their child's education, the school must not give up. In general, people will talk in confidence to people they trust. Building trust with parents is a crucial way to show that you understand and care about not only their child, but also about *them* and the struggles they may be facing as a parent.

As a teacher, you can make weekly—or, when necessary, daily—contact with the parents about the progress of their children at school and provide professional suggestions of ways they can assist their child's education. Be friendly and show compassion. When schools are more aware of circumstances involving the families, better communication will be established. If necessary, the school can organize the meeting before school hours or after. If the communication is important, make it work. Once a relationship is started, concentrate on building it up even further by reaching out with a sincere approach to help.

Some schools flourish in terms of parent-teacher relations, but many continue to flounder. Poverty-stricken families and poverty-stricken school districts are still searching for ways to make the connection work. One of the most important aspects to building trust is having parents that believe in you. Ask parents what might be holding them back; *listen* to their answers and show them empathy. Be persistent. Parents have to know that your caring is genuine and that the school is on their side. Learning the best way to communicate is by far the most underrated component of enhanced collaboration.

Whether you use email, text, or a more comprehensive classroom management system to engage with parents, you can improve parent-teacher communication with classroom technology. Because emails and texts are so quick to send, you can keep parents in the loop, whether through a weekly classroom newsletter or daily text updates about a student's progress. Parents will appreciate your professionalism and respect your efforts. When communicating, no matter the mode, choose your words carefully. Once you send a message, there is no getting it back. Words matter, tone matters, and a genuine love for the child and the parents, matter.

Meredosia-Chambersburg, the school district where the Link Up program originated, is also home to many poverty-stricken students and families, with over half of the student body eligible for free or reduced lunch. The school faces many roadblocks, but the Link Up program has been able to help many students in need.

For years, a fourth-grade boy had been dealing with severe emotional issues. From the time he entered kindergarten, teachers tried to intervene by contacting his parents, but the family ignored all calls for help. The family knew there was a serious problem, but for some reason they didn't want to confront it with school personnel.

Searching for answers and finding few, the school chose a popular teacher to Link Up with the boy and become his full-time mentor and family confidante. The teacher, over the years, had developed a good relationship with the boy's aunt who was a student at the high school. Using this connection, the teacher was able to connect with the boy's mother. After several phone calls and text messages, the mother felt comfortable enough to meet with the school.

When participating in the Link Up program, schools can choose to get matching Link Up bracelets. At the first parent-teacher meeting for that fourth-grade boy, the teacher gave the mother a bracelet that matched his and the student's: matching black rubber bracelets with white interlocking links. These matching bracelets made the mother feel like she was a part of something with her child, creating an immediate connection with the school.

Soon, the mother and teacher worked together to convene an IEP team—including psychologists, supervisors, and school staff—to create a plan for this boy's educational needs. For the first time, the boy had a plan and his future had purpose. He was given certain accommodations to help with his academics and specific techniques to use in controlling his behavior.

As an educator, you have the power and resources to help your students' parents get involved—even if that means enlisting the help of a mentor or other staff members. While the process can be long and difficult, the benefit to the student will be well worth the effort.

Takeaways for Teachers:

- When caregivers—including parents, grandparents, or any other guardians—get involved with a child's education, children become more motivated to do well in school.
- Parents might struggle to get involved with their children's teachers and schoolwork, especially if there is financial or emotional hardship in the family.
- Teachers can encourage parental involvement through making regular contact with guardians, showing them empathy, and keeping them up to date on school events.

NOTES

1. Kocayoruk, Ercan, (2016). Parental involvement and school achievement. *International journal of human behavior*, volume 2 issue 2, (2016) DOI: http://dxdoiorg/10.19148/ijhbs.65987

2. "Grandparents Raising Grandchildren in the United States: New Research into Characteristics and Challenges." August 3, 2020. https://apnews.com/press-release/business-wire/6291481d56654620b7ba65b13b4e7b72

3. Child Trends Databank. (2019). *Foster care.* https://www.childtrends.org/?indicators=foster-care

Section 3

WORKING WITH MENTORS

Chapter 10

Free Human Capital

What's in it for me? Sometimes, that might be a question you ask someone requesting a favor, or it might be what others say to you when you when you ask them for help. Regardless, the desire for compensation is everywhere. Parents promise their kids money for good grades. Teachers reward their students for good behavior with a movie. Society in general, feel like they should be rewarded for what should be expected behavior. To develop a sense of empathy, children need to learn that helping another person can be enough of a reward in itself.

THE VALUE OF STUDENTS

Similarly, all humans have inherent value and the potential to provide value to someone else without any compensation getting involved. The most valuable asset you have is with you for as long as school is in session, walking the halls while passing from one class to another, congregating at lockers, sharing a laugh about weekends past or the thought of an upcoming game.

Everywhere you look, you see young people with all sorts of strengths, interests, and desires. Watching them interact, you can tell that that some are full of confidence. Some, not so much. Regardless, there is value in all of them—every student is a hidden gem in their own right. Point these kids in the right direction with the right goals and you will see them share their value. They simply need a concrete plan developed by their school and shared with them.

Many high school-aged kids are searching for meaning in life. Looking for direction, a place to feel needed, or simply something to occupy their time. Many have big hearts and love to share—but for some, the only outlet they can identify for sharing their feelings and experiences is social media. While social media can be a great communicative tool, students need more than mass interactions through a phone; you can help them build one-on-one connections with others in their community.

WHAT IS FREE HUMAN CAPITAL?

Jill S. Reis, Regional Superintendent for multiple counties on the west side of Illinois, describes the ability to provide value to others as "free human capital." Students and teachers alike have an inherent value: their potential to help others. For many schools struggling with budget cuts, the emphasis here is on "free." Most schools need more counselors, psychologists, and social workers on staff—if they even have any to begin with. But in the meantime, you can make a difference using resources already available to you—without having to wait for someone else to approve a budget that may or may not ever increase.

Children in need are all over the map. Direction does not dictate need. From one coast to the other, every school has students who need an intervention.

In February of 2019, the original Link Up team from the Meredosia-Chambersburg school district traveled to Springfield, Illinois to present the mentoring program. Arriving with a solid sheet of ice covering the parking lot, made for a perilous trip into the St. Patrick Catholic School, which has been carrying out its educational mission since 1910.

The school serves students from all races, creeds, and religions from grades pre-school to grade five. The children that attend the school are

100 percent free-lunch eligible and come from homes considered high poverty.

Once inside, the team was greeted by a warm and gracious staff of loving administrators and teachers. The school was having an in-service in the afternoon for the teachers and the Link Up team was providing information about the life-changing mentoring program. After much discussion, the Link Up team learned of a high school right around the block from the elementary school. Access to free human capital was merely two minutes away.

Before the team left, staff at St. Patrick made a phone call to the principal at Southeast High School about the possibility of partnering the elementary and high school for the Link Up program. After the call, both the elementary and high school added instating the mentorship program to their agendas.

Springfield Southeast High School is a public high school with an enrollment of 1,220 students, with 68 percent of students classified as economically disadvantaged and a 74 percent graduation rate, ranking it in the bottom half of Illinois schools. The low graduation rate is the result of falling behind at an early age, which in most students' cases results from poverty.

USING FREE RESOURCES TO HELP
LOW-INCOME SCHOOLS

According to the US Department of Health and Human Services, education is one of the five social determinants of health.[1] Given the fact that a high school diploma is one of the basic necessities for employment and the attainment of higher education, lowering the school dropout rate is of extreme importance. Experts agree that home and school environments impact the likelihood of graduating from high school. Furthermore, children whose parents are not involved in their schooling are more likely not to finish high school.

Additionally, 26 percent of students who were not reading proficiently in 3rd grade and who lived in poverty for at least a year between

2nd and 11th grade dropped out or did not finish high school on time—compared to 9 percent for students with basic or below-basic reading skills who had never lived in poverty.[2]

A mentoring program cannot fix poverty, but it can improve how a child living in poverty views him or herself. A mentoring program can elicit more parental involvement. Mentors can help improve reading levels by providing opportunities for children to practice reading skills with guidance in a comfortable setting.

The Link Up Mentoring Program was planting seeds at Springfield Southeast High School and St. Patrick Catholic School, who were Linking Up to help change the dropout narrative. The two schools, physically two minutes apart, are no different than schools across the country. Southeast High School has 1,220 students ranging in age from 14–18: young men and young women looking for purpose and eager to help, just like the students in your school.

As mentioned in earlier chapters, the mentoring program is not for every single student. There are many students in every high school and certainly in Southeast High School as well, that lack the necessary qualities to properly mentor. However, there are plenty with the character traits needed to make a life-changing difference. Southeast High School has been right around the block from St. Patrick since 1967, and in 2019, these two schools finally tapped into the free human capital that had been walking their halls for half a century.

It's long overdue to use this valuable human resource. What resources are right around the block from you—or inside your school building?

NOTES

1. https://www.healthypeople.gov/2020/topics-objectives/topic/social-dete rminants-health/interventions-reso

2. Hernandez DJ. Double jeopardy: how third-grade reading skills and poverty influence high school graduation. New York: The Annie E. Casey Foundation; 2011.

Chapter 11

Preparing the Next Generation of Teachers

Back in the day, teaching school in a one-room building was not easy. You had several different ages of children from first grade through eighth grade. You were paid little, but you were respected by all. The teacher was in charge and the children were held accountable. The schoolhouse itself was used for Sunday church service and was the focal point for the entire community.

Many of the great and admirable traits of teachers 100 years ago are still found in buildings all over the world today. Teachers everywhere are still eager, dedicated, and looking to impart life-changing knowledge to children. However, some things have changed for teachers, which has placed public education in a precarious situation. Due to a frighteningly low number of college students entering the field of education, along with more and more teachers leaving for other jobs or retiring early, people are wondering what has happened. Why does teaching seem less desirable to some than it used to?

EFFECTS OF THE TEACHER SHORTAGE

According to research by the Economic Policy Institute, the teacher shortage could reach 200,000 by 2025, up from 110,000 in 2018.[1] This shortage is due to a variety of factors. Among them are pay, working conditions, lack of support, lack of autonomy, and the changing curriculum. Class sizes are rising, causing a detrimental effect on these outcomes. As the number of teachers' declines, class sizes have to increase to compensate.

Having more kids in a class can also affect teacher performance: with more children to monitor, more children's behavior that needs managing, and more assignments to grade, less time is available to give to each individual student. The pressure on teachers to obtain high test scores amps up stress further. It creates a vicious cycle, which is starting to snowball. The shortage is only set to increase unless something changes.

Teachers always seem to have a good sense of humor about the lack of pay when compared to other sectors with similar college credentials. The general public sometimes laughs off the pay gap by pointing to the "summers off" that teachers enjoy—forgetting to account for all the extra work teachers put in off the clock, including grading assignments and planning new lessons.

In addition to low pay, working conditions are in record decline. Lack of support and respect from the community is growing and teachers are wearing down. With so many districts cutting their budgets, teachers are left to spend their own money for classroom resources to make the classroom more appealing and beneficial to the student. Considering the college debt one would have to incur to become a teacher, combined with the promise of low pay and the likelihood of spending out-of-pocket money on classroom supplies, teaching doesn't seem financially beneficial to many members of Generations Y and Z.

Due to this teacher shortage, classroom leaders sometimes lack the necessary education and training in topics like pedagogy and classroom management. Many states and school districts are using citizens with any type of degree and placing them in charge of children. Many of them are great human beings, but it's yet another example of not fully meeting the needs of children.

How do we get back to a time when teachers were revered, respected? How do we find a new set of passionate teachers who will look forward to coming to school each day? How do we get the next generation excited about the possibility of becoming a teacher? There are plenty of candidates roaming the hallways all across the country. The Link Up Mentoring Program is the perfect place to foster a love of teaching within your students.

DISCOVERING PASSION THROUGH MENTORING

Over 15 million young men and women attend a high school near where they live: a treasure trove of talent and maybe some future teachers. The human connection that communities and schools are lacking live within the very school and community. Many of those walking the halls are "diamonds in the rough"—but not ever teenager can see their own potential.

Juniors and seniors in high school are beginning to think about their futures and their career paths. Some may be afraid to go into teaching, fearing the long hours and low pay—which is a valid fear to have! But some of these students may have a hidden passion for watching young people learn. Some may have a natural ability to connect with students and impart wisdom to them. As a teacher or administrator, you have the power to help these kids see teaching as an option for their future.

The Link Up program also gives high school students first-hand experience working with young people; through their daily duties, they can determine whether teaching is a path they want to pursue when they reach college.

A high school student hasn't been in an elementary room for many years—their thoughts and feelings about life will have dramatically changed since then. When a high school student becomes a mentor, they work under the supervision of their mentee's classroom teacher. In addition to gaining experience working with a child, the high school student can observe how a classroom teacher operates from an outside perspective.

During its first semester of operation, Charleston High School, on the eastern side of the Illinois—the second school to adopt the Link Up program—chose to connect eight high school students and eight children. At the end of the first semester, teachers and administrators from Charleston met with teachers and administrators from the Meredosia-Chambersburg school district—where the Link Up program originated—to discuss the program's success. Based on the program's success, Charleston decided to add more mentors for the next semester.

At the meeting, Charleston's cooperating principal reported that three of the high school girls in the mentorship program, who had never expressed interest in teaching prior to starting the program, were now all interested in pursuing teaching after high school. After quality time spent mentoring children and seeing the teacher impact lives, they were determined to be teachers, too.

Every school that has participated in the Link Up program has stories of teens who discovered their love for teaching while mentoring a child—but these stories are from a small sample size. Imagine the impact when incorporating a fraction of the 15 million high school students throughout the United States.

Takeaways for Teachers:

- Fewer people pursue teaching as a profession in the past few years, likely due to long hours, low pay, and stricter testing guidelines.
- If more young people don't enter the field of teaching, class sizes will have to keep increasing, which takes necessary attention away from individual students.
- An internship can give high school students a glimpse into the daily life of a teacher.
- Mentoring a younger student can help spark a passion for teaching in a teenager.

NOTE

1. https://www.epi.org/publication/the-teacher-shortage-is-real-large-and -growing-and-worse-than-we-thought-the-first-report-in-the-perfect-storm-in -the-teacher-labor-market-series/

Chapter 12

Identifying the Link Up Mentor

High-school-aged students need meaning in their lives. As mentioned in an earlier chapter, teens are searching for meaning on social media, but social media platforms are designed to provide users with temporary dopamine hits rather than prepare them for long-term accomplishments.

Dr. Abigail Marks, a clinical psychologist for teens, explains, "With the vast amount of information on the internet and social media, adolescents may feel like every choice they make—big and small—is an opportunity for failure. Even worse, they may fear that this failure is permanent."[1]

Social media sends the message that perfection is attainable and that falling short decreases a person's value. During adolescence, new stressors such as peer pressure, emerging sexuality, and fear of rejection can be very detrimental to the teenager's self-esteem. A *Journal of Adolescence* study revealed that teens' self-esteem improved with performing altruistic acts. The biggest increase in self-esteem came from helping people other than family or friends. "Helping a stranger is more challenging than assisting a friend, and when teens take this risk, they feel more competent" says Dr. Laura Padilla-Walker,[2] a psychology professor for Brigham Young University.

If not given an opportunity to contribute to a greater cause, teens' searches for meaning can lead to less than desirable behavior, like using drugs, bullying others, or acting out to get adults' attention. However, when teens *are* given the right opportunities and resources, they can contribute to a positive outcome in a child's life, adding purpose to their own life by proxy. Taking on a younger student as a mentee may be exactly what a teen needs to feel productive and valuable.

WHAT MAKES A GOOD MENTOR?

To become a strong mentor, a teenager needs to show the ability to be selfless: to demonstrate a sense of empathy and an ability to put their mentee's needs first. Employing selfless habits in a self-absorbed world can be a challenge. The debate about why humans are selfish is ongoing.

To an extent, high school kids are naturally selfish, at no fault of their own. According to *The Wall Street Journal*, teenage brains are still developing their ability to exhibit empathy; many humans don't finish developing the ability to view others' perspectives until age 21.[3]

Selfish behavior becomes worse during the teenage years, when they are trying to achieve independence. A teenager is focused inward while they struggle to find their own identity, which can result in thinking less about others and breeding conflict with peers and authority figures. Regardless, plenty of students walking the halls in school buildings have self-sacrificing tendencies, even if they don't know it yet. As an adult implementing a mentorship program, you have a responsibility to identify those qualities in your students and show confidence in their potential to be selfless.

RELIABILITY IS KEY

Selflessness can feel like a vague concept to identify; students at this age thrive when given specific expectations. A good mentor is one you can trust to meet those expectations. Trustworthiness comes along with another quality teens must exhibit: reliability.

Being present and punctual is one of the keys to exhibiting reliability and building trust. When people rely on you it's imperative that you consistently show up on time. In this case, a socially at-risk child is relying on their mentor to be prompt in arriving. The child in question looks forward to their mentor's arrival and they know exactly, to the minute, what time they're supposed to arrive.

Studies indicate that teens are often late because they don't like where they're going.[4,5] A teen who has a miserable time at school won't feel motivated to get there on time. The solution seems to be motivating and exciting teens; if they're looking forward to going somewhere, they won't procrastinate. Interested mentors must fully understand the impact that they could have on this child. They must become emotionally invested in their mentorship; they must *want* to be there. Once they make a connection with the child they are mentoring, they will want to attend in a timely fashion because they will feel the importance every day.

Back in 2018, one Link Up mentor was on the Meredosia-Chambersburg High School volleyball team. The team was playing an away game on a Tuesday night and arrived back home at around 11:00 p.m. After the game, her body was screaming, *Sleep in tomorrow!* However, just like every other weekday morning, she had a mentee who'd be waiting at 7:45 a.m.

When her alarm went off early that next morning, she struggled to get out of bed. But what got her moving was the thought of her mentee, a child she had counting on her. She got herself to school early and met up on time with her mentee.

She later shared her exhaustion and struggle to get out of bed with her teacher; but, she explained, she couldn't bring herself to disappoint the child. Because this mentor *wanted* to be where she was going (to meet up with her mentee), and because she had developed empathy for the child she was mentoring, she overcame the powerful desire for extra sleep.

Along with the importance of punctuality comes accountability. At one point at Meredosia-Chambersburg, two mentors were matched up with two children in the same classroom, where they met with their identified child at 7:45 every morning. Like clockwork, they were always on time.

Unfortunately, the classroom teacher was always running late and the kids were forced to meet in the hallway for most of the morning. The mentors were growing tired of the situation and asked the teacher for help. With permission from the classroom teacher, another teacher would let the students in the room. These students showed accountability when, instead of seeing the teacher's lateness as an insurmountable roadblock, they searched for solutions and asked for help. Because these mentors cared about the kids, they set a priority to meet with them in a comfortable location, their classroom, rather than the hallway.

TAP INTO THE NEED FOR INDEPENDENCE

Volunteering productively taps into a teen's innate desire to be independent. Teenagers are extremely busy with academics, extracurricular activities, sports, building relationships with friends, and planning for their futures. Sharing a few hours out of their busy schedule regularly for their school can be therapeutic for them. Many teens crave greater responsibilities and the chance to prove their independence to parents, teachers, and other authority figures. As an educator, you can seek out students who are showing a desire for greater independence; they could make a great mentor!

Identifying a Link Up mentor is an important decision for school personnel. The selection process is not scientific and involves a diverse range of students. Some are quiet and unassuming. Some are outspoken and confident in their own skin. Oddly, there will be students that you thought would fit perfect who are not interested in serving as a mentor. You'll also see more withdrawn students step up to the plate. As long as the students show the commitment to the program, they can benefit from Linking Up.

Takeaways for Teachers:

- A successful mentor is one who's ready to make a solid commitment.
- Reliability, accountability, and punctuality build a sense of trust between mentor and mentee.
- Mentors who are emotionally invested in the wellbeing of their mentee are more likely to keep their commitments even when other issues arise.
- Consider a variety of students as potential mentors; sometimes, students who are less outgoing or less involved in school activities are ready to step up to the plate!

NOTES

1. Fraga, Juli. "Helping Strangers May Help Teens' Self-Esteem." NPR. 13 January 2018. https://www.npr.org/sections/health-shots/2018/01/13/577463475/helping-strangers-may-help-teens-self-esteem

2. Ibid.

3. Shellenbarger, Sue. "Teens Are Still Developing Empathy Skills." The Wall Street Journal. 15 October 2013. https://www.wsj.com/articles/SB10001424052702304561004579137514122387446#:~:text=%22Cognitive%20empathy%2C%22%20or%20the,problem%2Dsolving%20and%20avoiding%20conflict.

4. Malik, Ladhani, and Bhamani. "Decreasing Student Tardiness through Strategic Reward System: an Action Research Report." *Abhinav,* 2016.

5. Maile, Simeon. "The Causes of Late Coming among High School Students in Soshanguve, Pretoria, South Africa." *Pedagogical Research*, 2017.

Chapter 13

Mentor Training

Kindness seems to be an innate trait for many, but for others, kindness can be a learned behavior. For some, showing kindness is easy and self-rewarding. For others, fully grasping the importance of sharing acts of kindness takes time, effort, and practice. People recognize kindness when they see it or feel it. The Link Up program has always maintained that showing compassion or kindness to an identified socially at-risk child doesn't require special training. This belief has proven true over the course of time; for most situations within the school, sharing compassion will suffice. However, certain challenges may arise that require mentor training.

INCLUDE MENTORS IN
EDUCATOR CONFERENCES

Throughout the school year, teachers are asked to attend faculty meetings, take part in team building activities, and appear at educational conferences. These events are designed to educate the teacher to better reach the children under their care. The education for the teacher helps them navigate through trying times during the school year. Leaning on each other and sharing information helps the individual teacher and the entire school. Including the mentor in these activities will go a long way in the success of the mentor and the Link Up program.

The sharing of educational materials and ideas has long been a bedrock of the public school system. Treating mentors as equals in the day-to-day educational process allows for consistent growth. This growth will allow for better results between the mentor and the mentee. With added knowledge comes confidence.

Teachers and mentors alike can achieve this knowledge and confidence at teacher conferences. These conferences occur once a year in school districts throughout the country and offer teachers an opportunity to learn from experts in a variety of topics. Presenters are selected by the conference administrators and assigned to specific rooms around the school's campus.

Teachers can request conference itineraries from their administrators to select the topic that will benefit them the most; many conferences will allow for teachers to attend three or four presentations during the day. In addition to the specific presenters, teachers have an opportunity to listen to keynote speakers that will hopefully inspire and uplift them for the duration of the school year.

With creative scheduling from the school's guidance counselor, the mentor could attend the conference and gain valuable knowledge. Selecting the appropriate break-out session would be up to the cooperating teacher of the mentor. Choosing the right workshop will help the mentor learn and communicate the learned material with their chosen mentee.

If a conference in your state contains programming or workshops about addressing the needs of students with low self-esteem, discussing the right and wrong ways to use social media, developing healthy habits, or any similar topics, see if you can work with the guidance counselors and administration to bring your mentors along as a field trip.

For the past five years, the Link Up program has been a featured presenter at the Quincy, Illinois Conference. The conference is held in early October each year and brings in over 2,000 teachers from the surrounding area. This valuable resource is used by teachers, administrators, classroom aides, and can also be used to educate/train Link Up mentors. Conferences like the one in Quincy are held throughout the country and will offer ample opportunity for all Link Up mentors to learn more about the socially at-risk child under their care.

SEEK PROFESSIONAL DEVELOPMENT OPPORTUNITIES

Teachers and administrators are constantly pursuing professional development opportunities that will help in the classroom and in the school district. In Illinois, teachers must accumulate 120 hours of professional development training every 5 years to renew their license. The Link Up program is a certified provider of professional development. In addition to attending local conferences, Meredosia-Chambersburg School District, the birthplace of the Link Up program, hosts teachers from around the state at the school to learn about mentorship.

Once again, through creative scheduling by the school's guidance counselor, the mentor can learn at the very school where they are providing mentoring help. In many schools, this is called a school improvement day and is a great time to involve the mentor. The mentor will not only learn from the presenter, but they will also learn from other teachers within the school that have years of teaching experience. See if your school is planning to host any professional development events and work with your administrators to get student mentors involved.

For schools to be compliant, teachers and staff are required to take yearly online tests to ensure they are keeping up to date with local laws and current methods. Meet with your administrators and guidance counselors to find the best way for your student mentors to take these online courses and tests as well. Some online course topics you may want your mentors to pursue include behavioral intervention, sexual harassment, active shooter response, student medical emergencies, substance abuse prevention, and most important of all, mandated reporter training.

This is a concrete and effective way to teach the mentor about topics that may come up throughout the course of a school day or year. By incorporating the teacher's conferences, school improvement days, and online testing, the mentor can be informed.

TRAIN MENTORS AS MANDATED REPORTERS

The Link Up program is an excellent opportunity for students who are interested in pursuing careers in health and human services. Being a student mentor is a great introduction into the world of social work, counseling, education, and health careers. Many of the children served by the Link Up program have been victims of abuse and or neglect. It is critical that the student mentor understands the role of a mandated reporter.

Each mentor should be provided information regarding mandated reporting. They should be prepared for what to watch and listen for. While as a student, they would not be expected to report directly to child and family services, they would be expected to report to their cooperating teacher or an administrator. These situations, while disturbing, do serve as an introduction to the reality of working in these careers.

Mandated reporting laws have been in effect in the United States since 1963, with all 50 states having laws by 1967.[1] Mandated reporter laws vary from state to state, with some being more comprehensive than others. The laws have changed significantly over time to strengthen protection of children. In their 2014 article for the *Villanova Law Review*, Leonard G. Brown III and Kevin Gallagher conclude that mandating that everyone reports abuse does not always prevent further abuse, but it does increase awareness of the problem.

The Link Up program works to develop advocacy skills in student mentors. Going forward in their careers, the ability to advocate for themselves and for others will build the framework for success both professionally and personally.

Takeaways for Teachers:

- Many of your mentors will already have an innate sense of kindness. Including them in professional development will foster this sense of kindness and teach them how to contextualize it.
- Talk to your school's administrators and guidance counselors about registering mentors for educational conferences in your state.
- Sign your mentors up for online mandated reporter training. Your mentors should report any situations of abuse to you, or to their faculty point of contact, and then you can pass that information along to child services.

NOTE

1. Leonard G. Brown III & Kevin Gallagher, *Mandatory Reporting of Abuse: A Historical Perspective on the Evolution of States' Current Mandatory Reporting Laws with a Review of the Laws in the Commonwealth of Pennsylvania,* 59Vill. L. Rev. Tolle Lege 37 (2014).

Chapter 14

The Mentor's Daily Tasks

The primary role of a Link Up Mentor is to serve the identified socially at-risk child placed under their care. First and foremost, the mentorship is about the child. The classroom teacher has identified this child for reasons that only they know; they will share as much as they can about the child with the mentor, and the mentor will work with the teacher to create a daily plan. The planning can change from day to day due to the needs of the child; sometimes, the child might be behind on some classroom work and need to complete it under the mentor's motivation. Other times, the child and mentor might read a book together.

ARRIVING AT SCHOOL

Until the child arrives for school, the mentor can assist the teacher with classroom chores that will help all the children, like classroom organization, bulletin board construction, or photo copying. Serving the teacher until the child arrives will always be part of a mentor's daily tasks. This element of the mentorship allows high school interns to understand the teaching profession behind the scenes.

BREAKFAST IS NECESSARY

When the child arrives at school, the first order of business is to make sure the child has eaten breakfast. If possible, no day will start without something to nourish the child. For many families, there are too many obstacles to providing a healthy morning meal each day. Tight budgets for low-income families and busy morning schedules can mean that students arrive at school hungry and not ready to learn.

If the school provides breakfast, but the child arrives late, the mentor should retrieve breakfast for them from the cafeteria. As a teacher or administrator, you can work with your school's cafeteria to identify which mentors are allowed to pick up breakfast for which students, which breakfasts are free, and any other concerns. Regardless, the identified socially at-risk student must start the day right. Breakfast will improve academic performance, remove hunger as a distraction, and improve overall morale of the child.

HOMEWORK HELP

The next order of business is to sit down and finish any work that's not done. Work completion is so important in building confidence and momentum for the rest of the day. Setting a positive tone early on will have a positive effect for the rest of the day. Self-confidence originates from the child's perception of their own competence. Family praise and applause will only build so much; the child needs to recognize their own accomplishments.

CATCHING UP THROUGH CONVERSATION

After breakfast and the completion of unfinished work, the mentor and child will share some time conversing. For some children, when they speak, no one listens. Their family may give them the appearance of listening, but it's not sincere or active. A socially at-risk child needs to be not only heard, but understood.

The mentor will not have access to technology that inhibits their ability to focus and listen. Also, in the process of listening the mentor is learning. Talking and listening is of great importance as it helps the child build a bond and develop trust with the mentor. Listening enhances the bonding in the relationship and builds the child's confidence. The mentor will pay attention to the thoughts, feelings, and behaviors of the child. Trying to incorporate eye contact is crucial and is the best way to establish communication.

READING TOGETHER

Based on the internship course description, the mentor has 90 minutes every day to make a positive impact on the socially at-risk child. Making the most of that time is critical in changing the present narrative of the child. Somewhere within the 90 minutes must include reading time. Reading for pleasure or shared reading can benefit a child's education, social and cognitive development, their wellbeing, and their overall mental health.

Because of the learning potential, the effects of reading on the child's development are vast and convey a multitude of benefits. As such, teachers and mentors are in a great position to ensure reading is a key part of children's daily routine. Mentors and mentees should find a location outside of the classroom to read, such as the hallway or library, so that the student doesn't become distracted by other activities in the classroom.

One teacher can only focus on so many children at a time, and when a student needs specific assistance and there isn't a teacher's aide, a Link Up mentor is there to serve. In today's classrooms of 30-plus students, at-risk students cannot always receive the one-on-one help they need with reading, which is a crucial building block of education.

Most successful readers have support at home and school, but the child who struggles to keep up lacks the support system. There is no greater feeling than hearing the improvement in a child's tone, fluency, and word recognition. At Meredosia-Chambersburg, student reading has accelerated since the Link Up program began; especially for one particular student.

Teachers brought concerns to the Link Up program about a girl falling way behind her peers in reading, which was affecting other aspects of school. Since entering the school at the beginning of first grade, she struggled with a profound stuttering problem. Now in fourth grade and falling even further behind, she needed some one-on-one help. The stuttering was having a negative effect on her confidence and her social skills. She had a feeling of embarrassment when asked to read out loud or talking in front of others—as a result, she felt discouraged from reading.

For most children, stuttering occurs during a number of activities at home, in play, or in school. This child was stuttering *only* at school, in front of peers, and during reading activities. Building confidence was the key, and the Link Up Mentoring Program stepped in.

This student was paired up with a high school girl. As an internship, the Link Up program worked with the school to adjust the high school student's schedule so she could go to the elementary school during reading time. The mentor and mentee went outside of the classroom and worked together on reading skills for the full semester.

Pulling the child out of the room for an entire semester gave the child so much confidence. With no one other than her mentor around, the child learned to do shared reading with her mentor. The confidence gained was not overnight—but over the course of the semester, her reading visibly improved.

Early on, the child was hesitant to read, but with the encouragement of the mentor, she became a confident reader. After a semester of reading with her mentor, the child was ready to read in front of her classmates. With a full classroom of students, her teacher, and most important, her mentor, she began reading out loud to her classmates. Not at grade level, but with the confidence of a seasoned reader. Her performance wasn't perfect, but the smile on her face showed a dramatic increase in confidence—and more importantly, it showed that she overcame her fear of reading.

Academic improvement and social skills go hand-in-hand. When this child was no longer afraid to read out loud, her love of reading—and her reading skills—improved. Having a safe space to work on her reading with a trusted mentor made all the difference.

Takeaways for Teachers:

- When implementing the mentorship program, work with counselors, administrators, and any other school officials in charge of scheduling to make sure the mentor and mentee have a devoted 90 minutes together each day.
- Mentors should make sure that each student has eaten breakfast, even if the school needs to work out an arrangement with the cafeteria.
- Mentors and mentees should work on schoolwork together. When a child has the previous day's work done, they no longer feel like they've fallen behind, and they can work on moving forward once again.
- Mentors should work on reading skills with their mentee. Their reading time doesn't have to feel like an academic activity; they can pick books they both enjoy and read together for pleasure in a pressure-free environment.

Chapter 15

Transportation from School to School

Turning 16 is a rite of passage that most kids relish. Getting behind the wheel and learning to drive has long been a dream for teenagers. Whether in their own car or a borrowed car from their parents, teenagers may feel older and more independent when they can travel on their own accord.

However, this experience is not the same for every teenager. Where a teenager lives will heavily impact when and where they drive. Rural areas offer less congestion on the roads and an easier way to get places. Metropolitan areas can be challenging and unsettling for the young driver. Finding the safest way to travel has always been a top priority for families and schools.

The Link Up program is concerned as well; when high school students need to meet up with their elementary-school-aged mentees, the program needs to ensure that teens can transport themselves safely and efficiently. Planning for safe travel for all mentors should be a priority for all participating school districts.

For many teenagers, travel will not be an issue. For instance, at Meredosia-Chambersburg, a combined school of K–12 students, transportation for the mentor is not a concern; teen mentors simply walk from the high school side to the elementary school side of the building. In the United States there are 15,804 combined schools that would allow mentors easy access to the identified socially at-risk child.[1] Sharing the same campus makes the Link Up program an easy assimilation for the guidance counselor, classroom teacher, and the identified mentor. Scheduling is more convenient and the time spent traveling will be spent in the classroom instead of on the road.

In many instances, even though the school is not combined, they still share the same physical campus. Frequently, the high school student can see the elementary building from where the high school is situated. This too, makes for seamless and less stressful travel. In addition to combined schools and schools that share the same physical campus, there are schools that are simply blocks away. As was mentioned in an earlier chapter, when you see one school, there's likely another right around the block. Once again, although still a concern, transportation to and from the school is easily managed. The Link Up program has identified many schools that share the same town or zip code and are only separated by a few miles: a driving time of fifteen minutes or less with little traffic on the roads.

In some schools or districts, the option to provide school transportation for Link Up mentors is also an alternative. If the need is there for multiple mentors, the school could set up morning and afternoon transportation that takes the mentors to and from each school. Many schools now have smaller utility type buses that would work perfectly for the Link Up program. Bus transportation directors and guidance counselors should work together to make the times work for the mentors and other timely features within the framework of a traditional school day. In many cases, this commute would not take much time, but would be infinitely important for the children receiving services.

These methods may work well for students in suburban and rural settings but may not work for students attending school in a large city. If your school is located in a city like New York, Los Angeles, or Chicago, you may find yourself with a new set of transportation challenges, which you should work with your school's administrators to overcome.

Perhaps the biggest concerns for safety arise in school districts that are located in high crime areas. Schools may be close enough together to walk back and forth, but if that walk is not safe, walking is not a viable option. Public transportation may even be dangerous in some areas.

Again, school districts will need to be creative. For example, in the state of Illinois, Public Act 100-1142 expands a school district's ability to provide free transportation to students who would otherwise have to walk through areas of criminal gang activity.[2] The school district then receives reimbursement from the State Superintendent of Education. The Illinois State Board of Education encourages school districts to create planned school routes that offer protection to children. School districts are encouraged to collaborate with local engineers and law enforcement agencies to create planned school routes.

The make-up of each school will ultimately determine the overall planning needed to ensure safe travel. Making sure the mentor has arrived safely at the assigned school would require communication between the two schools. The mentor should sign in when they reach their destination and the elementary school should notify the high school. Signing out would follow a similar plan. High school students traveling for different school functions is not foreign for school districts, but for some districts, it will take strategic planning to secure safe trips to and from the assigned school.

Takeaways for Teachers:

- The location of your school, size of your district, and population density of your neighborhood will factor into the methods you use to transport mentors to and from mentees each morning.
- If your school is located in an area with high crime rates, see if your state offers any reimbursements for setting up safe transportation or any programs that allow you to collaborate with local law enforcement.
- If your high school mentors have their own cars and licenses, they may be able to transport themselves each morning.

- Unless your school is one K–12 building, make sure your mentors sign in with the main office when they arrive at the elementary school every morning to ensure safety.
- Work with your school's administrators to determine the safest and most time efficient plan of action based on your school's individual needs.

NOTES

1. Riser-Kositsky, Maya. "Education Statistics: Facts About American Schools," *Education Week,* June 16, 2020. edweek.org/ew/issues/education -statistics/index.html

2. Illinois State Board of Education (2020). https://www.isbe.net/ transportation

.

Chapter 16

Modeling Behavior

Frankly, perfect parenting doesn't exist. Parenting is one of the more challenging jobs for an adult to navigate. Children, by all accounts, present unique characteristics that test the very sanity of parents. Good parenting results from the ability to recognize mistakes and make adjustments.

For teachers, identifying children raised with sound parenting and consistent admirable mannerisms is easy. However, teachers can also identify children with poor parenting and less than admirable mannerisms. With the advent of recent technology, uninvolved parents now have more ways to avoid spending time with their kids, such as giving them an iPad with child-friendly games.

Educators have noticed in the past 5–10 years that socially at-risk children are showing up in classrooms at alarming rates. Teachers talk about it, but finding a solution can be difficult. This influx of at-risk students demands attention, which is why writing this book and sharing the mentoring program is so important. Teachers across the country can see this enormous potential in children, but because of social dysfunction in the home the child is trapped and looking for help. The teacher, with 30 other students in the room, would love to give some extra attention, but may lack the time or resources.

PARENTS ARE THE FIRST ROLE MODELS

The socially at-risk child can come from a multitude of backgrounds. The reality is that children may witness dangerous behavior from their parents, which is often compounded by the fact that often, the family lacks resources to meet the child's basics needs. Children will struggle to meet their full academic and social potential without the basic necessity of proper nutrition—yet many children living in the United States go hungry. In many rural areas, public transportation is not available. How can a parent go to a school function without transportation? How can that parent seek routine medical attention for their child without a way to get there?

These children, who grow up to be students, endure so much at a young age that socially endangers their future. Poor modeling as a parent becomes all the child knows and results in similar behavior by the child. Physical and verbal threats from parents are common, which teaches the child to act out at an early age.

One day at Meredosia-Chambersburg, the birthplace of the Link Up program, school had just been dismissed at 3:30. Teachers still had work to do; for one teacher, that work involved a meeting with a student's father. The young student was acting out in class and showing aggression toward other students. His behavior was causing him to fall behind academically, and the teacher was concerned for his future. The father showed up at the front entrance to the school to meet the teacher, a classroom aide, and his son. What happened next was eye-opening for the teacher and classroom aide.

The father, the teacher, the classroom aide, and the eight-year-old boy were standing at the entrance to the school when the father became enraged at his son. The father grabbed his son by the shirt collar with closed hands, picked him up, and pinned him up against a brick wall. He then yelled into the child's face, "What the fuck is wrong with you?" The teacher interceded and told the father to calm down. The father put the boy down, but immediately left the school with the boy in tow.

The teacher was shaking with fear and sadness. She reported the incident to the school principal for further discussion. The principal took down all the information and placed it on the school board's monthly agenda. With all the information collected, the principal recommended the father be banned from the school's premises for one calendar year. The school board agreed and notified the family.

The school took appropriate measures to provide a safe environment for the boy and all other students enrolled at the school. For the classroom teacher, the issue would not go away. The student became angry at his teacher and everyone he encountered at school. He continued to fight with classmates and refused to act in an orderly manner within the room. His grades suffered and concern gripped the teacher. The teacher confided with the Link Up program, which found a mentor for the student.

Before this student had a mentor to model behavior for him, his main example had been his father. This father had modeled verbal and physical violence as a response to anger; as a result, the child had begun to adopt that behavior himself. When a student is struggling, finding them a new role model can make a huge difference.

FINDING THE RIGHT ROLE MODEL

Everyone in the school—teachers, students, and staff—believed in the Link Up Mentoring Program, but not everyone was able or willing to volunteer for it. Teaching can be so stressful; each teacher knows their limits and employs strategies to make the best of each day. When one man heard the learned about this eight-year-old boy's struggles, he decided that he had the time and the energy to make a difference. The high school shop teacher volunteered to be this boy's mentor.

Every morning, the shop teacher and the boy would gather in the second-grade classroom from 7:45–8:20. The two would talk about the previous day, and they slowly developed a trusting and caring relationship. The shop teacher encouraged the boy to complete any homework he hadn't yet finished. Once the boy finished his work, he could work on a puzzle or read a book with his mentor. Day after day, the two became more trusting of each other and the results started to show in the classroom. As a mentor, the shop teacher always arrived on time, employed active listening skills, and gave his full attention to the student.

As their relationship grew, other students began wanting the shop teacher's attention. Soon, a group of boys were putting puzzles together with the shop teacher—who everyone thought was super cool—each morning. The young boy, who had previously shown aggression toward his classmates, was now making friends and working on puzzles with them. The shop teacher even took the kids on trips to the shop class to see what to expect when they get older. With consistency, discipline, and unwavering commitment, the boy was able to trust and believe in a male role model once again.

Parenting was hard enough before, but now, with social media dictating the start and ending of each day, it's become even harder. Kids want attention and they want someone to listen. Some kids overcome poor parenting and adjust to school without much problem. But for those in social jeopardy, it's important to have a plan in place. The Link Up program puts teachers, high school students, and staff in position to help.

HOW TEENS MODEL BEHAVIOR
FOR YOUNGER CHILDREN

High school students in particular play an important role in the Link Up Program. Elementary children look up to older kids and want to someday be like them. Boys and girls alike see themselves playing sports, going to dances, getting a job, or securing a driver's license. All children need to see high school students in an environment where they can model appropriate behavior. Displaying timely mannerisms in a disciplined and consistent manner is key to learning proper behavior. Following directions, listening, and not interrupting within the classroom setting is so important for kids to see.

For the socially at-risk child, it's even more important. Falling behind in school, academically and socially, at an early age becomes an overwhelming challenge. The child's future can be saved with proper modeling and interventions at an early age. Many times, the potential is there, but outside influences keep it from flourishing.

SETTING EXPECTATIONS FOR MENTORS

Because high school students can be incredible role models for younger kids, setting expectations for them is imperative. Teenagers need to know what behaviors they should model for their mentees and which to avoid.

Here are some guidelines that the Link Up program sets for teen mentors:

- The high school mentor will model passion and inspire the child to achieve. Mentors can model passion by talking to their mentee about their own activities and accomplishments, whether in sports, music, or school. However, mentors must be careful to keep the focus on the child and not to emphasize their own accomplishments in a way that intimidates the child.
- The mentor will display a commitment to the child and will not let them down. This commitment includes arriving on time each day.
- The mentor will help the child overcome obstacles and build confidence.
- The mentor will model selflessness. Selflessness includes listening actively to everything the child has to say, refraining from interrupting, and participating in activities the child enjoys.

Displaying selflessness is the most important component to being a good mentor. The child feels a real connection because there is nothing to interfere. Quality time in the classroom every day, without interruption, will enable the child to regain lost confidence and hopefully reach their given potential.

Takeaways for Teachers:

- When students display erratic or aggressive behavior, see if the parent is the source.
- When parents model violent or threatening behavior, students may need a new role model to set an example.
- Teachers and high school students alike can make great mentors for a student in need.
- Teen mentors need to make sure they're always modeling productive behavior for the child.

Section 4

AS YOUR PROGRAM GROWS

Chapter 17

Listen, Love, and Learn

One of the greatest gifts that people inside the walls of a school building can give to a child is to listen. Involved staff and students pay close attention to what children are saying. They are conscientious about all things surrounding the life of children under their care. Listening is truly one of the great obligations of love, an obligation that every school representative owes a child.

Listening takes patience and time. To listen actively, you must *want* to listen. Active listening requires both parties to understand one another. Sometimes with children, that's easier said than done. Teachers, with 30 children wanting their complete attention at the same time, have it more difficult than most. Wanting to actively listen doesn't always translate in the classroom.

Socially at-risk children frequently come from environments where active listening doesn't take place. When active listening is lacking, children often struggle to build a bond of trust with their family members. Children may not always remember what their parents say to them, but they do remember how it makes them feel.

Active listening is especially important for socially at-risk children who are constantly learning how to navigate the world by taking cues from those around them. Engaging in conversation with socially at-risk children, patiently listening, and allowing them the time to express themselves at their own pace creates a safe place for them to speak up and find their own voice, which will be very important in their coming years.

Many children have a chaotic home life. Unfortunately, parents are often distracted by difficult relationships, work problems, financial difficulties, and mental health issues. A stressed parent may turn to social media, video games, or other solitary pastimes to escape the reality of their situation. Without meaning to, parents tune their kids out, and those kids notice.

Non-communicative parents may cause children to give up and turn inward with their feelings and thoughts. Children may begin to feel invisible, like they have no impact on others. When socially at-risk children learn early on that their thoughts, feelings, and opinions have value, they no longer feel invisible. They are more likely to continue to share ideas and feelings well into their secondary school years.

WHY MENTORS NEED ACTIVE LISTENING SKILLS

If a child is identified as socially at-risk, they will need a listening ear in their life sooner rather than later. Having a friend, confidant, or mentor to listen to them will help with building their self-esteem. Starting a mentoring intervention at an early age makes it a normal part of the child's day. The child feels worthy of receiving attention; they'll learn that what they have to say matters.

The regular interaction with the child gives them practice in dealing with the school day and the outside world. Sharing quality time helps them develop positive social relationships. The child learns that a conversation involves not only speaking, but listening. Learning that relationships involve give and take teaches cooperative problem solving, how to be a good friend, and that sometimes, walking away from a situation is okay. More importantly, children learn the importance of asking for help when needed.

Promoting this interaction every day enables the mentor to learn from the child. Children, by nature, are creative and naturally think outside the box. Too often, adults dismiss children's ideas due to their age and inexperience, claiming that the child's idea is unrealistic or unimportant.

However, children's young minds have a lot to offer. Maybe the kid who likes to color in a puppy picture with green crayons will become an artist. Maybe the kid that likes stacking their pencils and markers will become an engineer. The difference between a child who pursues these dreams and one who gives up is often whether an adult is there to listen and take them seriously.

Socially at-risk children frequently have issues both inside and outside the classroom. Establishing a loving relationship between mentor and at-risk child will directly lead to improved behavior in the classroom. When the child knows you *see* them and *hear* them, it becomes easier to guide them toward more appropriate behavior in school.

Listening, loving, and learning are all benefits shared between mentor and mentee. The mentor is in a great position to step back and see the bigger picture of their mentee's environment. However, the mentor needs to remember that they don't know everything, either.

Mentors should view their role as one where they learn from the child: by asking the child questions and listening to their answers, the mentor should learn about the child's interests, personality, sense of humor, likes and dislikes, and more. Through listening, mentors can learn to identify their mentee's strengths and weaknesses and figure out the best ways to give their mentee advice.

For the high school student that steps in to mentor, the lessons learned will transfer to bigger things later in life; many of the same skills are applicable in college and the workplace. While a mentoring relationship is first and foremost to benefit the mentee, the mentor has just as much to gain in experience, confidence, and knowledge.

THE IMPACT OF A LISTENING MENTOR

By third grade, Charlie—a student at Meredosia-Chambersburg Elementary School—was out of control; he cursed at his teacher, refused to do any schoolwork, and attacked other kids on the playground. His home life was chaotic: he hadn't spoken to his father in years, and his mother frequently left him home alone. The odds of Charlie dropping out of high school one day seemed fairly high. The probability of legal problems, jail time, and substance abuse was also high.

One day, Charlie's mom pulled him out of school for a trip to see his dad. Charlie, unaware of where exactly he was going, recalls feeling suspicious and uneasy. They arrived in town and headed to the local courthouse. Charlie's dad had been arrested and brought into court for not paying child support. Charlie, sitting in the courtroom, watched as his dad was brought in handcuffed and legs shackled. Charlie's mom wanted to get back at the dad by taking him along to see him shackled.

Charlie couldn't believe what he was seeing and began to cry. Even though he didn't really know his dad, it was a sight he wanted to forget. After Charlie's teachers and administrators learned about his trip to the courthouse, the Link Up program intervened and started providing a mentor for Charlie. With no male role model in his life, the school assigned Charlie a high school Eagle Scout as his mentor.

The two started meeting and their relationship grew. The mentor, Eric, was proud of his work; he and Charlie met for 90 minutes every morning, and Eric's focus was on listening. Eric listened to Charlie's problems. He listened to what Charlie had to say and what he was interested in. As it turned out, Charlie was really interested in Eric's Eagle Scout work.

Eric taught Charlie some of the lessons he learned from scouting—so Eric helped Charlie sign up for Cub Scouts, providing him with an outlet for all of his extra energy. Soon, Charlie's behavior in class improved, his relationship with classmates improved, and his self-esteem reached historic levels. Another mentoring success story to share, but so many more to go. When a mentor spends a devoted time every morning listening to a child and learning about their interests, that child feels important.

As your own mentorship program grows, consider practicing active listening with your mentors. Host a training session after school where mentors practice active listening skills with one another and discuss how they can employ those techniques with their mentee. If your program has a budget—or if you plan to fund-raise—consider bringing in a communication expert to conduct an active listening workshop with your mentors. If your mentors meet during the school day for an internship class, consider devoting a class period to active listening skills.

Regardless of the specifics of your school's program, find a way to emphasize active listening with your mentors as they grow.

Takeaways for Teachers:

- Children want their ideas to be heard and taken seriously.
- Active listening is a necessary skill for a mentor—and anyone else who works with children—to have.
- Mentors should approach meetings as a way to learn more about their mentee. Their focus, especially in the beginning, should be on asking the child questions rather than trying to impart knowledge.

Chapter 18

The Door Is Always Open

Hundreds of years have passed since a child's learning came primarily from home. Parents were responsible for their child's education. If money was available, families would hire tutors to educate their children. The importance of education has always been understood as vital for the person and for society. The advent of public school has created an important force for equality: every child, regardless of financial or socioeconomic status, is entitled to an education.

Public schools have open doors for everyone that falls within the school's boundaries. No stipulations are made for income, skill level, or social status. With an open-door policy, schools are challenged by overcrowding, frequent dropouts, and numerous discipline issues. Some districts have significantly more upheaval than most, but never close their doors.

The school doors remain open for all children. Children may frequently move in and out of school districts for many reasons. Some children have parents that are migrant workers. Others move due to changes in their parents' relationship such as divorce. For those children living in poverty, the move may be the result of their parents looking for more affordable housing or even eviction.

For various reasons, children often move in with a grandparent or family member. For children in the foster care system, there are laws that protect their rights to remain in their school district. The Fostering Connections Act is a federal law that requires agencies to work with schools to provide educational stability. Schools are required to provide transportation for these students. This act passed in 2008 and has brought much needed attention to the importance of school stability for children in foster care.[1]

Homeless children are also protected by law. The McKinney-Vento Act provides educational stability for homeless children by giving them the right to remain in their school district while being homeless and up to the end of the academic year after they obtain permanent housing.[2]

While it is wonderful that we have school stability protection for homeless children and those living in foster care, many children still lack protection. Research has shown that children who change schools frequently experience lower reading and math achievement.[3] Each move is associated with a decline in social skills and the results appear to be cumulative.[4] Furthermore, frequent moves often result in emotional and behavioral problems. Devastatingly, these frequent moves increase the dropout rate of students.

At the Meredosia-Chambersburg School, it is fairly common for students to enroll mid-year or to come back and forth from school to school. The students affected by the constant upheaval seem almost immune to the uncertainty in their life. Even though they appear in control of their emotions, these students are often experiencing a heavy torment of uncertainty inside.

The staff at Meredosia-Chambersburg is used to dealing with incoming and outgoing students. A few years ago, one particular boy had recently moved from the district and was planning to return and re-enroll. Everyone loved the boy and was excited to hear he was coming back to their school. The boy's classmates were happy and eager to see him once again. The teacher in charge of his care was looking forward to making a difference in his education.

He arrived at school on a Wednesday and had a pretty productive day, smiling and laughing with his classmates and getting his work done. The school day came to an end and everyone went home. Everyone that went home on Wednesday came back on Thursday except that boy. He made it *one day* and was off to another family and another school. The staff felt lost once again, but once again they left the doors open for his potential return.

As an educator, especially one running a mentorship program for at-risk kids, you will need to be ready for the reality that a student may leave the school district and return periodically, especially if they come from an unstable home environment.

There are educational options for children outside of public school. In recent years, homeschooling has become an option for many families. With escalating violence in some schools, homeschooling can be an attractive choice. According to the National Center for Education Statistics (NCES), the number of homeschooled children in the United States increased from 850,00 in 1999 to approximately 1.7 million in 2016.[5] Homeschooling requires great commitment and time.

Many of the children identified in this book as socially at-risk have been pulled from the public school system to be taught by parents. These parents often blame the public school system for their child's poor academic and/or social success. On the other side, public school systems often recognize these parents as being unengaged in their child's education. Pulling their children from school out of anger, without researching and understanding what it takes to successfully homeschool, can lead to children becoming even further behind.

Public schools see this problem every year; watching children fall further behind is often incredibly disheartening for a teacher. The solution here is to work with parents to become more active in their child's education. In chapter 9, this book discussed the importance of parental and caregiver involvement in a student's life. As your mentorship program grows, make sure that you are involving parents in their child's development. A meeting among teacher, parent, child, and mentor can go a long way.

In addition to homeschooling, there are private schools for families to pursue. Private schools provide another option and have shown to be effective. Their focus is different from public schools and it comes with a higher cost. The option to attend a private school is often not an option for socially at-risk children due to the cost of tuition. According to National Private School Review, the average yearly tuition in the United States is $9,944 for elementary school tuition and $14,821 for high school tuition.[6] The highest private school tuition currently in the United States can be found in Litchfield County, CT. It is a staggering $45,000 annually. With these barriers, success for most children will always remain in the hands of the public school system where they live.

School choice has become the mantra for all other schooling outside the public school setting, including online schooling (COVID-19 has generated a lot of interest), vouchers, tax-credit programs, and educational scholarships. Everyone has a solution to the growing problem inside and outside the traditional school building.

About 80 percent of all children attend public schools based on where they live. The rest have chosen an alternative route to their education. The 80 percent that attend public schools are given ample chance to succeed if their parents will provide proper guidance.

A portion of the 80 percent, primarily socially at-risk children, needs public schools to survive. Millions of socially at-risk children are solely dependent on public schools to provide an environment for their education and growth. Public school educators must stay the course and fight for the children left to figure it out for themselves.

This remedy will be found by incorporating the small army of teenagers in public high schools nationwide. This small army will report for work every day, support the cooperating teacher, love the identified child, and help remedy the malaise on our watch. Society needs selfless leaders and the Link Up program is ready for action. One thing is for certain: when a child moves into the district, the doors will be open.

Takeaways for Teachers:

- As your program grows, you may have to deal with children moving in and out of the district. Make sure these students feel welcome if or when they return to your district.
- Parents often want to be involved in their children's education, even if they seem dissatisfied with the public school district.
- If parents show interest, make sure to keep them updated on their child's progress within the mentorship program. Let them know how their child has progressed since getting to know their mentor.
- Public schools are a place where students should always feel welcome. Use your mentorship program to create a welcome and supportive environment for students who need it most.

NOTES

1. American Bar Association, Children and the Law (2020) Retrieved from https://www.fostercareandeducation.org/AreasofFocus/EducationStability.aspx

2. School House Connection (2020). Retrieved from https://www.schoolhouseconnection.org/mckinney-vento-act/.

3. Coley, R. & Kull, M. (2016). Retrieved from https://www.macfound.org/media/files/HHM_Brief_-_Is_Moving_During_Childhood_Harmful_2.pdf

4. Ibid.

5. Grady, S. (2017). A Fresh Look at Homeschooling in the U.S. Retrieved from https://nces.ed.gov/blog

6. Average Private School Tuition (2020.) Retrieved from https://www.privateschoolreview.com/tuition-stats/private-school-cost-by-state

Chapter 19

Combating Teacher Burnout

Workplace stress occurs in many professions and often leads to burnout. As this book has discussed, teachers are already under a lot of pressure from the various roles they must uphold in a child's life. Creating a mentorship program, while ultimately beneficial to the children involved, does have the potential to create additional stress for you as a coordinator as well as for other teachers involved. Keeping your own stress in check and avoiding burnout will be crucial. This chapter will discuss some of the causes of workplace stress and teacher burnout and the ways you can overcome it.

WHAT CAUSES STRESS?

Jobs are a major source of stress for adults, according to the American Psychological Association's annual stress survey.[1] Not all stress is harmful; stress in small amounts can improve our problem-solving skills and can help us prepare for important life events.

During times of extreme stress, your heart and respiratory rates increase and your muscles tense as your body enters fight or flight mode. Usually after the event, your stress level returns to normal and your body functions also return to their usual state. In contrast, long-term exposure to work-related stress can affect mental and physical health.

Repeated activation of the body responding to stress can disrupt bodily functions and increase the possibility of disease. Workplace stress can cause high blood pressure, insomnia, and a weakened immune system. This type of stress may contribute to obesity and heart disease.[2] Unfortunately, people dealing with excessive stress often turn to unhealthy life choices to help cope with this stress. Examples of these unhealthy behaviors include overeating, eating unhealthy foods, and abusing alcohol or drugs.

Work-related stress takes a toll on mental and emotional well-being. Chronic stress has been associated with anxiety, depression, short temper, and difficulty concentrating.[3] According to the National Institute on Mental Health,[4] 18 percent of adults residing in the United States suffer from anxiety, although the actual number is estimated to be much closer to 30 percent due to many people, especially men, neglecting to report their mental health struggles.[5]

According to *Psychology Today*,[6] depression can often result from the indirect effects of stress. For instance, job stress often keeps people from pursuing healthy coping strategies. Stress can act like a snowball, creating more stress as it lowers a person's mood and puts them in a worse state of mind.

Work stress can also harm the overall environment of a group working together. Workplace stress creates conflicts between coworkers which creates additional conflict in other areas. Loss of productivity, absenteeism, and job turnover are all impacted by a work environment that is steeped in stress day in and day out.

WHAT CAUSES BURNOUT?

Career burnout results from repeated stress in the workplace.[7] Research has shown that burnout is correlated with many physical health problems, including death at an age younger than 45.[8] Symptoms of job burnout include exhaustion, pessimism, and a loss of commitment to your work. Employees often become emotionally detached from their work, leading to feelings of inadequacy and less productivity.[9]

The teaching profession from grades K–12 is often wrought with emotional exhaustion and teacher burnout.[10] Dealing with misbehaving students is exhausting. Classroom behavior, nationwide, has become a primary factor for increased levels of stress placed on the classroom teacher. Not only is the teacher suffering, but the students are feeling the stress as well. This classroom atmosphere negatively affects their ability to perform at appropriate levels.

Stressful classrooms affect test scores and overall classroom morale. Bad behavior within the classroom is not exclusively acting-out behavior, but also the act of not paying attention and daily refusals to listen and learn. The amount of time spent on the unruly student takes away from productive teaching time and classroom learning. When this happens every day, wasted classroom time leads to all students falling farther behind in the curriculum, leaving the teacher feeling inadequate and self-conscious.

HOW BURNOUT AFFECTS TEACHERS

Unfortunately, many public school classrooms are suffering from this type of dysfunction. This classroom dysfunction is creating undue stress and teacher burnout at alarming rates. One teacher at Meredosia-Chambersburg Elementary, though compassionate about her students and passionate for her work, began to experience this type of burnout as well. Dreading going to work every day was taking its toll on her passion for teaching. While she tried to be upbeat, her eyes and quivering voice said otherwise. This teacher was already dealing with other health issues and was not handling the additional stress with much success.

In this teacher's mind, each day presented a new opportunity. She never quit trying, but by the end of each day, she was mentally and physically exhausted. Making it to the end of the year seemed highly unlikely. Fortunately, with caring coworkers and a proactive administration, she found a solution in the form of working with paraprofessionals.

Enter any public school building and you will find caring teachers with big hearts. You will also find the same characteristics in a teacher's aide or paraprofessional. Meredosia-Chambersburg has an abundance of selfless paraprofessionals that are willing to help with any assignment. One paraprofessional in particular was assigned to help the classroom teacher mentioned above regain some stability in her classroom dynamics. Over time, the two began to work as one and a steady improvement could be seen in the morale of the teacher and her students. Helping with daily classroom activities from scheduling to clerical duties, this paraprofessional was invaluable.

COPING WITH STRESS AND BURNOUT

Just as socially at-risk students can benefit from a mentor relationship, teachers too need a support network of coworkers and administrators to help them face new and stressful challenges. One of the core concepts behind this book and behind the Link Up Mentoring Program is that people are stronger when they have others to rely on, whether adult or child, teacher or student.

Teacher stress, absenteeism, and longevity are a real issue. Meredosia-Chambersburg is an example of a school district that is making teachers a priority. A productive learning environment requires teachers that feel supported and valued. Teachers, like all humans are individuals. Each teacher handles the stress of the job differently.

Many studies have examined how burnout affects teachers of different backgrounds and demographics.[11] Gender plays a role in burnout: female teachers report a higher level of emotional exhaustion, while male teachers report higher levels of depersonalization and inefficacy as a causative factor for burnout.

Teaching is an emotionally intense career. On any given day, teachers must deal with a span of emotions from joy to rage. Unfortunately, due to the increase of school violence, fear is an emotion teachers can experience as well. Students today have very complicated family and social situations. How to fairly treat children who have such difficult life situations without excusing bad behavior or laziness takes a huge toll on a teacher's emotional and intellectual capacity.

The dynamics of each classroom differ as well. Some classrooms are simply harder to maintain, whether due to number of students or the makeup of the students in the room. Disruptive student behaviors in the classroom may or may not be a reflection on the teacher's ability to control the classroom. Some teachers internalize the poor classroom behavior along with student's lack of attention and perceive themselves as failures. Whatever the reason is for poor classroom behavior, it can leave the teacher with feelings of frustration and anger.

Frustration is an easier emotion to talk about with colleagues than anger. Anger can be considered unprofessional; a teacher may be worried about being judged by colleagues when they reveal their feelings of anger. Feeling angry is a very normal emotion, though, and should be expected in certain situations. The way that the teacher *chooses to deal with their anger* will determine their level of professionalism.

First-year teachers are often unprepared for the emotional work involved in teaching. New teachers face the fear of not being respected by their students or colleagues. Furthermore, a new job often leaves a teacher feeling anxious about whether they're prepared to make quick classroom management decisions. Given the fact that most first-year teachers are much younger than the students' parents, confrontational parents can be a source of angst.

New teachers should be prepared for the range of intense emotions they will encounter while teaching so that they can enter the profession prepared with a realistic view and not an overly optimistic view of teaching.[12] The Link Up program gives the mentor an opportunity to view both the good and bad emotions that teaching brings.

Emotional support from colleagues goes a long way to help battle teacher burnout. Teachers need a safe forum where they can talk through their emotions without fear of judgement. Emotion-focused and problem-focused coping has been useful in easing burnout.[13] An emotion-focused coping strategy could be as simple as talking about your feelings with another teacher. Problem-focused coping may include finding assistance like a paraprofessional in the classroom.

Some teachers may find avoiding their problems or suppressing their emotions to be the easiest way to deal with stress; however, this type of disengagement leads to higher levels of burnout. Administrators and all members of the faculty should adopt an atmosphere of inclusiveness and openness where all members can honestly express their concerns and emotions.

The classroom of children and their teacher should always be the primary focus in every district. Much like the Link Up mentoring program, classroom paraprofessionals are looking for ways to help. Placing a sincere focus on high school mentors and paraprofessionals is a win for the teacher, the children, and the school.

Alleviating some of the stress consuming today's teachers, young and old, will provide a clear path toward more learning and stability in classrooms everywhere. Just like teenage mentors, thousands of caring citizens live in every school district in the country. Many of these caring citizens don't wish to have a four-year degree with massive amounts of college debt, but they do love kids and if asked, would love to help their local school. Selfless acts will begin the trek toward strong schools. Link Up mentors and paraprofessionals are a great place to start.

Takeaways for Teachers:

- As your mentorship program grows, you may find yourself with additional work and more stress on your plate. Taking care of yourself and avoiding burnout is important.
- Repeated daily stress can lead to burnout. Because teaching can be an emotionally and intellectually exhausting career, teachers are at a high risk for burnout.

- Just as students can benefit from a mentorship, teachers can benefit from the connections they have with their coworkers. Asking for help is crucial.
- Teaching aides and paraprofessionals can be an invaluable resource for teachers struggling with oncoming burnout.

NOTES

1. American Psychological Association (2018). Retrieved from https://www.apa.org/topics/work-stress#:~:text=When%20stress%20persists%2C%20it%20can%20take%20a%20toll,high%20blood%20pressure%20and%20a%20weakened%20immune%20system.

2. Ibid.

3. Ibid.

4. National Institute of Mental Health, "Any Anxiety Disorder." Retrieved 27 November 2020, https://www.nimh/nih.gov./health/disorder/any-anxiety-disorder.shmtl

5. Anxiety Statistics, Facts, and Information (2020). Retrieved from https://www.anxietycentre.com/anxiety-statistics-information.shtml#:~:text=Anxiety%20has%20become%20the%20number%20one%20mental%20health,reported%20high%20levels%20of%20anxiety%20in%20the%20workplace.

6. Alice Boyes, PhD. "Why Stress Turns into Depression." *Psychology Today*, March 7, 2013. https://www.psychologytoday.com/us/blog/in-practice/201303/why-stress-turns-depression

7. Salvagioni DAJ, Melanda FN, Mesas AE, Gonzalez AD, Gabani FL, Andrade SMd (2017), "Physical, psychological and occupational consequences of job burnout: A systematic review of prospective studies." PLoS ONE 12(10): E0185781. https://doi.org/10.1371/journal.pone.0185781

8. Ibid.

9. Ibid.

10. Chang, Mei-Lin. "An Appraisal Perspective of Teacher Burnout: Examining the Emotional Work of Teachers." *Educational Psychology Review* (2009) 21: 193-218.

11. Ibid.

12. Ibid.

13. Ibid.

Chapter 20

Now More than Ever

What is the effect of a pandemic on a society? How does it affect a child, their parents, their family? There are a plethora of questions surrounding the COVID-19 pandemic. While understanding the total effect of the pandemic may take many years, many educators already feel its negative impact on education. When COVID-19 arrived in the United States, remote learning was the answer to providing education while protecting children, families, and teachers. Unfortunately, educators and administrators did not have time to organize well. This coupled with the fact that many children did not have internet access led to high levels of frustration for educators, administrators, families, and especially students. Society soon came to realize just how important school life was for children.

HOW MASS REMOTE LEARNING
AFFECTS CHILDREN

For children, school is a safe place. When you live in a home with abusive personalities, school is a place where you don't have to fear what might be coming next. Often, it is a teacher that discovers that a child is being abused. According to the Department of Health and Human

Services, teachers and educational staff are responsible for reporting one in five cases of abuse.[1] This is higher than any other category of reporter.

In the Washington, DC area, the Center of Disease Control (CDC) reported a 62 percent decrease in the reporting of child abuse during mid-March through April 2020 compared to the same period in 2019.[2] Unfortunately, during this same time frame in 2020, there was a more severe presentation of abuse in children treated in emergency rooms. This, of course, was during the same time frame that schools were closed during the pandemic.

In addition to academics, schools provide children opportunities to learn social skills and to develop interpersonal relationships. While in school, children learn how to behave in groups and how to develop relationships with children and adults outside of their family. Children learn how to trust and how to ask for assistance, but they also learn how to find answers for themselves and how to help others. This type of learning requires in-person contact and is nearly impossible with distance learning.

The development of these social skills is important for all children but significantly important for those children who have behavioral disorders. Those children with behavioral disorders need special plans to facilitate the development of social skills.

Schools also provide access to social workers and mental health providers that children may not receive outside of school. School counselors are experts at recognizing mental trauma in children that parents or guardians, who may be working through their own mental health issues, may not be able to recognize. The CDC reports that 14 million children between the ages of 9 and 17 have mental health conditions.[3] Without in-school learning, many children lose access to the mental health services they need.

School-aged children are not as likely to get sick from COVID-19, but their mental health is at risk. According to *The Lancet*, "post-traumatic stress scores of children and parents in quarantine were four times higher than those not quarantined."[4]

Socially at-risk students, who are already facing tough odds, now find themselves at risk of falling even further behind. School closures have impacted all students, but especially the child that was already struggling and behind their peers. The closure of schools across the United States during the pandemic for in-person learning has been devastating.

Interrupted learning at all levels has made the challenges that schools face even more daunting. According to the Northwest Evaluation Association, just being out of school for the summer causes students to lose some of their newfound knowledge: on average, after third grade, students lose about 20 percent of the previous year's gains in reading and 27 percent of that year's gains in math just over the summer.[5] The months of distance learning followed by summer likely left children critically lacking academically.

Reopening in the fall of 2020 was met with strict guidelines that forced school districts everywhere to adapt. With the country still in panic mode and no end in sight, many schools were forced to decide the best path forward for the children under their care. Some schools opted for remote learning even though they knew it was best, educationally, to be in person. Some schools chose to offer a hybrid approach that gave each family a choice. Some schools offered four days in person and one day of remote. Many of these plans reduced the time spent at school because of all the stipulations placed on schools by health experts. In person, by all accounts, even with the mandates was best, but the learning was still lacking.

During the period of distance learning, being away from friends, teachers, and staff has taken a serious emotional toll. Getting off the bus, wearing a mask covering their face to protect others and hoping to stop the spread of the virus. We are uncertain what emotional toll wearing a face mask, having their temperature taken and being screened for COVID-19 every school day will have on students and faculty. Further research will be needed to determine the final conclusion. For some students, school may not feel safe. Children are not exempt from stress. Listening and learning from your teacher, also wearing a mask, makes for a challenging day. Many children are wondering, "What is going on? Will my family be safe?"

MENTORING DURING A PANDEMIC

The results of the pandemic and its overall impact on education on children of this generation will take years to fully understand. Public schools are the lifeblood of a free society trying to mold the next leaders. The COVID-19 pandemic has left the schools needing mentors for children now more than ever.

If you're reading this book in 2021 during the pandemic, the natural response might be, "This program sounds like a good idea, but I'll wait to pursue it until the pandemic is over." The problem is that *during* the pandemic, children need positive role models outside of their own homes more than ever before. Starting up a mentoring program while schools are socially distanced—or even fully virtual—might feel impossible. But here are some tips to make it happen.

Put Technology to Good Use. Throughout this book, you've seen how much teenagers use social media, smart phones, and the internet. Why not encourage them to use their phones for mentoring? While nothing quite matches a face-to-face interaction—and after the pandemic ends, your top priority should be implementing the mentorship program face-to-face—you can still get those relationships forming. If your school is completely virtual, see if you can set up a daily FaceTime or Zoom call between your mentors and their mentees.

Find Safe Locations. Some places allow people to meet face-to-face while still socially distancing. If your school has an in-person component right now, see if you can reserve an hour in the school gym, on a sports field, or in the cafeteria. Set up markers to station mentors and mentees a minimum of six feet apart and require masks. While this experience won't quite match the original intent of the program, those meetings may still be crucial for the child in need.

The COVID-19 pandemic is a time of uncertainty and instability; right now, children require a consistent interaction with someone they can trust. Though implementing or growing this program during a pandemic is certainly a challenge, it can also be life-changing—now, more than ever.

Takeaways for Teachers:

- Many students are feeling unprecedented levels of stress during the pandemic.
- Implementing or growing a mentorship program is more of a challenge with virtual and socially distanced learning—but you should still try.
- Virtual or socially distanced mentor meetings can be a feasible alternative while keeping students safe—both physically and emotionally.

NOTES

1. https://www.childwelfare.gov/pubPDFs/educator.pdf

2. https://www.cdc.gov/coronavirus/2019-ncov/community/schools-childcare/reopening-schools.html

3. Ibid.

4. Brooks SK, Webster RK, Smith LE, Woodland L, Wessely S, Greenberg N, et al. The psychological impact of quarantine and how to reduce it: rapid review of the evidence. 2020;395(10227):912–920. doi: 10.1016/S0140-6736(20)30460-8.

5. Kuhfeld, Megan. "Summer learning loss: What we know and what we're learning." *Northwest Evaluation Association*, July 2018. https://www.nwea.org/blog/2018/summer-learning-loss-what-we-know-what-were-learning/

Author's Note

My Life-Changing Link

Teaching school can best be summed up as unpredictable. Each day seems to bring a new challenge and there is usually little warning. If you teach long enough, you will have plenty of examples to share and one or two stories to tell. Some of the tales can be sad and make you want to cry. Some bring you so much joy that you can't wait to share with anyone that will listen. Some can be so unbelievable that you hesitate to share for fear that people won't believe you. For some, a life-changing story is the best of all. Who wouldn't want to share a story that changed not only your life, but the life of a student in your class? Well, here is my life-changing story: the story that inspired not only this book, but the entire Link Up Mentoring Program.

On October 9, 2014, a young man and his mother arrived at my school to meet the principal, a supervisor from the local special education cooperative, and the boy's new teacher—me. I'll never forget the moment I saw that boy for the first time: he was thin, undernourished, and unkempt. His mother revealed that her son had also been diagnosed with autism. Due to the student's placement on the autism spectrum and the high level of assistance he required, the principal and I were unsure whether he needed to be in a special needs school instead. However, the supervisor from the special education cooperative was confident that he would thrive in our school, so we enrolled him.

From that day forward, he was bussed to the school from his home 30 minutes away. As a teacher, I had worked with students on the autism spectrum before; however, this student presented his own unique set of challenges, including being unable to share his emotions verbally.

Some of the challenges that make autism difficult are part of the school environment. For a child with sensory dysfunction, the loud noises, bright lights, and other sensory input of a normal schoolroom can be overwhelming. Verbal expression is an expectation for students but may be almost impossible for some children with autism. Executive functioning, the ability to plan and execute while using time management skill, can also be difficult for those with autism. It can be difficult for autistic kids to tell playful teasing from bullying, or to recognize sarcasm or humor.[1] Changes in routines, schedules, and expectations are particularly hard for children with autism to manage. All in all, the average classroom can be a challenging experience for the child with autism.

My new student had many of these traits—he often felt sensory overload and struggled to convey his thoughts and emotions out loud. However, my first concern was making sure that this child was properly nourished. Because many students at my school come from impoverished backgrounds, not everyone has access to healthy foods at home. This student had that challenge coupled with his genuine fear of certain foods. When I first met him, he was severely underweight: only 87 pounds at 5'10.

I soon learned that the school lunch would not be a viable option for this student: some of the foods in our cafeteria made him shake with fear. Trying to communicate this was a challenge, but through trial and error, we were slowly finding our way. The student's mother indicated that he'd be willing to eat peanut butter, apples, and drink chocolate Boost—so that became his specialized meal every day. Although it was originally out of my comfort zone, I started feeding this student five spoonfuls of peanut butter every day for a year. During that school year, the student gained 30 pounds and was slowly becoming healthier.

In addition to the lack of nutrition, the student was lacking commonly applied grooming. When he first arrived at our school, this student had long, dirty fingernails and long hair that he wouldn't let his mother cut. After building up trust with this student, I helped him with trimming his nails, and our school, thinking outside the box, invited a local hairdresser to come into the room for a personal haircut. Not only was the child receptive, but he enjoyed all of the attention. He also enjoyed the compliments from classmates who liked his new haircut.

With his nutrition reaching a solid point, the school began focusing on his cardio. Because I used to coach my high school's football team, I started working with the student on his hand-eye coordination. Using his love for basketball, we would hit the gym for ball drills and a little weight training. The kid was a natural and would show his talented shooting and ball handling to anyone in the gym. The school purchased him a 3-wheeled bike for exercise and for a chance to get outside. He very rarely saw sunlight when he was home. He was gaining weight, confidence, and friends. He looked good, felt good, and loved coming to school. He couldn't tell you how much he enjoyed the attention, but his expression on his face said it all.

With nutrition, grooming, and cardio improving, the school needed to get a better handle on his medicine. The child's mother worried that his current medication was further limiting his ability to express emotions. She asked me if I'd come with her to visit her son's doctor. On the drive over, I asked the mother for directions to the appointment, and the student responded with words—one of the first moments I'd seen him talk out loud.

After arriving at the doctor's office, the mother asked me to go inside and explain to the doctor what the school was seeing during the day. Meeting the psychiatrist and his wonderful nurse set the stage for the rest of the year.

After the psychiatrist listened to the boy's experiences in school, he decided to change up his medication. That first visit turned in to 10 more, leading to a connection among the medical team, the school, and the child's family. During the visits, I shared everything about the routine of the day. The doctor, concerned about the cost of feeding the child, slipped me a 50-dollar bill to buy some chocolate Boost and peanut butter. Although not asked for, it was greatly appreciated.

After each visit, our team was growing in faith with one another and we could feel the momentum building. Not only was the child's self-esteem soaring, but his mother, raised in a foster home, not knowing her own parents, was building self-esteem, too. It was beautiful to see.

Of course, not every day was progress. Some days presented unique challenges. One of our most trying days will live with me forever. This boy and his mother had an appointment with his general practitioner for a routine health check. Up to this time, he was functioning well at school and home. He was gaining strength and confidence each day. Everyone at school could see his development and the entire school was proud to play a part in his improvement. All of this optimism came to a screeching halt after his visit with his general practitioner.

The next day at school, the boy was not himself, and I was curious as to why. He was so weak that he couldn't hold his head up. He was resting his head on the table and struggling to keep his saliva inside his mouth.

Extremely worried, I took him to the nurse to check his vitals; everything seemed to be okay. We made it through the day, but the next day was the same. I grew even more frantic and reached out to the boy's psychiatrist for some answers. I called the clinic, but the psychiatrist was out of town on business in New York City.

Refusing to settle, I asked the office staff for help. I was given the psychiatrist's cell number and I contacted him for help. After the doctor consulted with others, he determined that the boy had been taken off a certain medication after his general practitioner visit, and he was unable to function as a result.

The medication was an honest mistake, but that day had been terrifying for everyone that loved this boy. After one last trying day, he was back on his appropriate medicine and he was back to his old self. That day, I learned that working together, communicating always, and loving as one will always work.

Finding that life-changing link can come at anytime and at any place. That fateful day, when the school enrolled the child, with his mother at his side, was the day I found my life-changing link. What I didn't tell most people was that, around that time, I was considering retiring from my teaching career. I'd been teaching for over two decades and I was getting tired of the grind. However, when I chose to stick around for that student, I found more meaning in my career, and to this day, I'm still a teacher with no plans to retire.

The links created in this situation inspired me to not only continue teaching, but also start something bigger—in this case, the Link Up Mentorship Program. This child found strength in those around him—not just me or his mother, but also his doctors, the school administration, and most importantly, the intersection of us all working together. I found the strength to continue my teaching career from this boy, his mother, and the other teachers around me. This child's progress made me realize that true power comes in the connections we make with those around us—and the more we can connect to and rely on one another, the more strength we'll all find collectively.

In life, there are life-changing links everywhere you go. You won't see them if you walk around with blinders on or your nose stuck in your phone. People are looking for someone to step up, engage the moment, and help make their life better. At first, I thought this child needed me to be his Link of Strength; but as it turned out, I needed him even more! Look for a life-changing link and become that link for someone else.

—Cary Knox

NOTE

1. Rudy, Lisa, (2020) https://www.verywellhealth.com/why-school-is-so-ch allenging-4000048

About the Author

Cary Knox is a nonfiction author from Roodhouse, Illinois. Cary has been in public education for 30 years. During this time, Cary has focused his attention on children with learning disabilities and those identified as socially at-risk. Cary's vast experiences in these areas compelled him to write the book, *From Selfies to Selflessness: Improving Student Self-Esteem through Mentoring*.

In addition to his work in education, Cary has published 10 pieces of inspirational wall art that gives glory to those who provide unconditional love and strength. Cary is represented by literary agent, Cyle Young. With Cyle's help, Cary has secured a contract to write a 40 day devotional, dedicated to the athletes and teams from the University of Illinois. Cary is an avid Fighting Illini fan and loves sharing the Illini's history.

Cary and his wife, Kellie, are the proud parents of four and the grandparents of six. They currently reside in Hillview, Illinois, on the family farm.